Mometrix
TEST PREPARATION

Common Core Grade 10 English Language Arts Secrets Study Guide

Dear Future Exam Success Story

First of all, **THANK YOU** for purchasing Mometrix study materials!

Second, congratulations! You are one of the few determined test-takers who are committed to doing whatever it takes to excel on your exam. **You have come to the right place.** We developed these study materials with one goal in mind: to deliver you the information you need in a format that's concise and easy to use.

In addition to optimizing your guide for the content of the test, we've outlined our recommended steps for breaking down the preparation process into small, attainable goals so you can make sure you stay on track.

We've also analyzed the entire test-taking process, identifying the most common pitfalls and showing how you can overcome them and be ready for any curveball the test throws you.

Standardized testing is one of the biggest obstacles on your road to success, which only increases the importance of doing well in the high-pressure, high-stakes environment of test day. Your results on this test could have a significant impact on your future, and this guide provides the information and practical advice to help you achieve your full potential on test day.

Your success is our success

We would love to hear from you! If you would like to share the story of your exam success or if you have any questions or comments in regard to our products, please contact us at **800-673-8175** or **support@mometrix.com**.

Thanks again for your business and we wish you continued success!

Sincerely,
The Mometrix Test Preparation Team

Need more help? Check out our flashcards at:
http://MometrixFlashcards.com/CCSS

Written and edited by the Mometrix Exam Secrets Test Prep Team
Printed in the United States of America

TABLE OF CONTENTS

Introduction

Thank you for purchasing this resource! You have made the choice to prepare yourself for a test that could have a huge impact on your future, and this guide is designed to help you be fully ready for test day. Obviously, it's important to have a solid understanding of the test material, but you also need to be prepared for the unique environment and stressors of the test, so that you can perform to the best of your abilities.

For this purpose, the first section that appears in this guide is the **Secret Keys**. We've devoted countless hours to meticulously researching what works and what doesn't, and we've boiled down our findings to the five most impactful steps you can take to improve your performance on the test. We start at the beginning with study planning and move through the preparation process, all the way to the testing strategies that will help you get the most out of what you know when you're finally sitting in front of the test.

We recommend that you start preparing for your test as far in advance as possible. However, if you've bought this guide as a last-minute study resource and only have a few days before your test, we recommend that you skip over the first two Secret Keys since they address a long-term study plan.

If you struggle with **test anxiety**, we strongly encourage you to check out our recommendations for how you can overcome it. Test anxiety is a formidable foe, but it can be beaten, and we want to make sure you have the tools you need to defeat it.

Secret Key #1 – Plan Big, Study Small

There's a lot riding on your performance. If you want to ace this test, you're going to need to keep your skills sharp and the material fresh in your mind. You need a plan that lets you review everything you need to know while still fitting in your schedule. We'll break this strategy down into three categories.

Information Organization

Start with the information you already have: the official test outline. From this, you can make a complete list of all the concepts you need to cover before the test. Organize these concepts into groups that can be studied together, and create a list of any related vocabulary you need to learn so you can brush up on any difficult terms. You'll want to keep this vocabulary list handy once you actually start studying since you may need to add to it along the way.

Time Management

Once you have your set of study concepts, decide how to spread them out over the time you have left before the test. Break your study plan into small, clear goals so you have a manageable task for each day and know exactly what you're doing. Then just focus on one small step at a time. When you manage your time this way, you don't need to spend hours at a time studying. Studying a small block of content for a short period each day helps you retain information better and avoid stressing over how much you have left to do. You can relax knowing that you have a plan to cover everything in time. In order for this strategy to be effective though, you have to start studying early and stick to your schedule. Avoid the exhaustion and futility that comes from last-minute cramming!

Study Environment

The environment you study in has a big impact on your learning. Studying in a coffee shop, while probably more enjoyable, is not likely to be as fruitful as studying in a quiet room. It's important to keep distractions to a minimum. You're only planning to study for a short block of time, so make the most of it. Don't pause to check your phone or get up to find a snack. It's also important to **avoid multitasking**. Research has consistently shown that multitasking will make your studying dramatically less effective. Your study area should also be comfortable and well-lit so you don't have the distraction of straining your eyes or sitting on an uncomfortable chair.

The time of day you study is also important. You want to be rested and alert. Don't wait until just before bedtime. Study when you'll be most likely to comprehend and remember. Even better, if you know what time of day your test will be, set that time aside for study. That way your brain will be used to working on that subject at that specific time and you'll have a better chance of recalling information.

Finally, it can be helpful to team up with others who are studying for the same test. Your actual studying should be done in as isolated an environment as possible, but the work of organizing the information and setting up the study plan can be divided up. In between study sessions, you can discuss with your teammates the concepts that you're all studying and quiz each other on the details. Just be sure that your teammates are as serious about the test as you are. If you find that your study time is being replaced with social time, you might need to find a new team.

Secret Key #2 – Make Your Studying Count

You're devoting a lot of time and effort to preparing for this test, so you want to be absolutely certain it will pay off. This means doing more than just reading the content and hoping you can remember it on test day. It's important to make every minute of study count. There are two main areas you can focus on to make your studying count.

Retention

It doesn't matter how much time you study if you can't remember the material. You need to make sure you are retaining the concepts. To check your retention of the information you're learning, try recalling it at later times with minimal prompting. Try carrying around flashcards and glance at one or two from time to time or ask a friend who's also studying for the test to quiz you.

To enhance your retention, look for ways to put the information into practice so that you can apply it rather than simply recalling it. If you're using the information in practical ways, it will be much easier to remember. Similarly, it helps to solidify a concept in your mind if you're not only reading it to yourself but also explaining it to someone else. Ask a friend to let you teach them about a concept you're a little shaky on (or speak aloud to an imaginary audience if necessary). As you try to summarize, define, give examples, and answer your friend's questions, you'll understand the concepts better and they will stay with you longer. Finally, step back for a big picture view and ask yourself how each piece of information fits with the whole subject. When you link the different concepts together and see them working together as a whole, it's easier to remember the individual components.

Finally, practice showing your work on any multi-step problems, even if you're just studying. Writing out each step you take to solve a problem will help solidify the process in your mind, and you'll be more likely to remember it during the test.

Modality

Modality simply refers to the means or method by which you study. Choosing a study modality that fits your own individual learning style is crucial. No two people learn best in exactly the same way, so it's important to know your strengths and use them to your advantage.

For example, if you learn best by visualization, focus on visualizing a concept in your mind and draw an image or a diagram. Try color-coding your notes, illustrating them, or creating symbols that will trigger your mind to recall a learned concept. If you learn best by hearing or discussing information, find a study partner who learns the same way or read aloud to yourself. Think about how to put the information in your own words. Imagine that you are giving a lecture on the topic and record yourself so you can listen to it later.

For any learning style, flashcards can be helpful. Organize the information so you can take advantage of spare moments to review. Underline key words or phrases. Use different colors for different categories. Mnemonic devices (such as creating a short list in which every item starts with the same letter) can also help with retention. Find what works best for you and use it to store the information in your mind most effectively and easily.

Secret Key #3 – Practice the Right Way

Your success on test day depends not only on how many hours you put into preparing, but also on whether you prepared the right way. It's good to check along the way to see if your studying is paying off. One of the most effective ways to do this is by taking practice tests to evaluate your progress. Practice tests are useful because they show exactly where you need to improve. Every time you take a practice test, pay special attention to these three groups of questions:

- The questions you got wrong
- The questions you had to guess on, even if you guessed right
- The questions you found difficult or slow to work through

This will show you exactly what your weak areas are, and where you need to devote more study time. Ask yourself why each of these questions gave you trouble. Was it because you didn't understand the material? Was it because you didn't remember the vocabulary? Do you need more repetitions on this type of question to build speed and confidence? Dig into those questions and figure out how you can strengthen your weak areas as you go back to review the material.

Additionally, many practice tests have a section explaining the answer choices. It can be tempting to read the explanation and think that you now have a good understanding of the concept. However, an explanation likely only covers part of the question's broader context. Even if the explanation makes perfect sense, **go back and investigate** every concept related to the question until you're positive you have a thorough understanding.

As you go along, keep in mind that the practice test is just that: practice. Memorizing these questions and answers will not be very helpful on the actual test because it is unlikely to have any of the same exact questions. If you only know the right answers to the sample questions, you won't be prepared for the real thing. **Study the concepts** until you understand them fully, and then you'll be able to answer any question that shows up on the test.

It's important to wait on the practice tests until you're ready. If you take a test on your first day of study, you may be overwhelmed by the amount of material covered and how much you need to learn. Work up to it gradually.

On test day, you'll need to be prepared for answering questions, managing your time, and using the test-taking strategies you've learned. It's a lot to balance, like a mental marathon that will have a big impact on your future. Like training for a marathon, you'll need to start slowly and work your way up. When test day arrives, you'll be ready.

Start with the strategies you've read in the first two Secret Keys—plan your course and study in the way that works best for you. If you have time, consider using multiple study resources to get different approaches to the same concepts. It can be helpful to see difficult concepts from more than one angle. Then find a good source for practice tests. Many times, the test website will suggest potential study resources or provide sample tests.

Practice Test Strategy

If you're able to find at least three practice tests, we recommend this strategy:

Untimed and Open-Book Practice

Take the first test with no time constraints and with your notes and study guide handy. Take your time and focus on applying the strategies you've learned.

Timed and Open-Book Practice

Take the second practice test open-book as well, but set a timer and practice pacing yourself to finish in time.

Timed and Closed-Book Practice

Take any other practice tests as if it were test day. Set a timer and put away your study materials. Sit at a table or desk in a quiet room, imagine yourself at the testing center, and answer questions as quickly and accurately as possible.

Keep repeating timed and closed-book tests on a regular basis until you run out of practice tests or it's time for the actual test. Your mind will be ready for the schedule and stress of test day, and you'll be able to focus on recalling the material you've learned.

Secret Key #4 – Pace Yourself

Once you're fully prepared for the material on the test, your biggest challenge on test day will be managing your time. Just knowing that the clock is ticking can make you panic even if you have plenty of time left. Work on pacing yourself so you can build confidence against the time constraints of the exam. Pacing is a difficult skill to master, especially in a high-pressure environment, so **practice is vital**.

Set time expectations for your pace based on how much time is available. For example, if a section has 60 questions and the time limit is 30 minutes, you know you have to average 30 seconds or less per question in order to answer them all. Although 30 seconds is the hard limit, set 25 seconds per question as your goal, so you reserve extra time to spend on harder questions. When you budget extra time for the harder questions, you no longer have any reason to stress when those questions take longer to answer.

Don't let this time expectation distract you from working through the test at a calm, steady pace, but keep it in mind so you don't spend too much time on any one question. Recognize that taking extra time on one question you don't understand may keep you from answering two that you do understand later in the test. If your time limit for a question is up and you're still not sure of the answer, mark it and move on, and come back to it later if the time and the test format allow. If the testing format doesn't allow you to return to earlier questions, just make an educated guess; then put it out of your mind and move on.

On the easier questions, be careful not to rush. It may seem wise to hurry through them so you have more time for the challenging ones, but it's not worth missing one if you know the concept and just didn't take the time to read the question fully. Work efficiently but make sure you understand the question and have looked at all of the answer choices, since more than one may seem right at first.

Even if you're paying attention to the time, you may find yourself a little behind at some point. You should speed up to get back on track, but do so wisely. Don't panic; just take a few seconds less on each question until you're caught up. Don't guess without thinking, but do look through the answer choices and eliminate any you know are wrong. If you can get down to two choices, it is often worthwhile to guess from those. Once you've chosen an answer, move on and don't dwell on any that you skipped or had to hurry through. If a question was taking too long, chances are it was one of the harder ones, so you weren't as likely to get it right anyway.

On the other hand, if you find yourself getting ahead of schedule, it may be beneficial to slow down a little. The more quickly you work, the more likely you are to make a careless mistake that will affect your score. You've budgeted time for each question, so don't be afraid to spend that time. Practice an efficient but careful pace to get the most out of the time you have.

Secret Key #5 – Have a Plan for Guessing

When you're taking the test, you may find yourself stuck on a question. Some of the answer choices seem better than others, but you don't see the one answer choice that is obviously correct. What do you do?

The scenario described above is very common, yet most test takers have not effectively prepared for it. Developing and practicing a plan for guessing may be one of the single most effective uses of your time as you get ready for the exam.

In developing your plan for guessing, there are three questions to address:

- When should you start the guessing process?
- How should you narrow down the choices?
- Which answer should you choose?

When to Start the Guessing Process

Unless your plan for guessing is to select C every time (which, despite its merits, is not what we recommend), you need to leave yourself enough time to apply your answer elimination strategies. Since you have a limited amount of time for each question, that means that if you're going to give yourself the best shot at guessing correctly, you have to decide quickly whether or not you will guess.

Of course, the best-case scenario is that you don't have to guess at all, so first, see if you can answer the question based on your knowledge of the subject and basic reasoning skills. Focus on the key words in the question and try to jog your memory of related topics. Give yourself a chance to bring the knowledge to mind, but once you realize that you don't have (or you can't access) the knowledge you need to answer the question, it's time to start the guessing process.

It's almost always better to start the guessing process too early than too late. It only takes a few seconds to remember something and answer the question from knowledge. Carefully eliminating wrong answer choices takes longer. Plus, going through the process of eliminating answer choices can actually help jog your memory.

Summary: Start the guessing process as soon as you decide that you can't answer the question based on your knowledge.

How to Narrow Down the Choices

The next chapter in this book (**Test-Taking Strategies**) includes a wide range of strategies for how to approach questions and how to look for answer choices to eliminate. You will definitely want to read those carefully, practice them, and figure out which ones work best for you. Here though, we're going to address a mindset rather than a particular strategy.

Your odds of guessing an answer correctly depend on how many options you are choosing from.

Number of options left	5	4	3	2	1
Odds of guessing correctly	20%	25%	33%	50%	100%

You can see from this chart just how valuable it is to be able to eliminate incorrect answers and make an educated guess, but there are two things that many test takers do that cause them to miss out on the benefits of guessing:

- Accidentally eliminating the correct answer
- Selecting an answer based on an impression

We'll look at the first one here, and the second one in the next section.

To avoid accidentally eliminating the correct answer, we recommend a thought exercise called **the $5 challenge**. In this challenge, you only eliminate an answer choice from contention if you are willing to bet $5 on it being wrong. Why $5? Five dollars is a small but not insignificant amount of money. It's an amount you could afford to lose but wouldn't want to throw away. And while losing $5 once might not hurt too much, doing it twenty times will set you back $100. In the same way, each small decision you make—eliminating a choice here, guessing on a question there—won't by itself impact your score very much, but when you put them all together, they can make a big difference. By holding each answer choice elimination decision to a higher standard, you can reduce the risk of accidentally eliminating the correct answer.

The $5 challenge can also be applied in a positive sense: If you are willing to bet $5 that an answer choice *is* correct, go ahead and mark it as correct.

Summary: Only eliminate an answer choice if you are willing to bet $5 that it is wrong.

Which Answer to Choose

You're taking the test. You've run into a hard question and decided you'll have to guess. You've eliminated all the answer choices you're willing to bet $5 on. Now you have to pick an answer. Why do we even need to talk about this? Why can't you just pick whichever one you feel like when the time comes?

The answer to these questions is that if you don't come into the test with a plan, you'll rely on your impression to select an answer choice, and if you do that, you risk falling into a trap. The test writers know that everyone who takes their test will be guessing on some of the questions, so they intentionally write wrong answer choices to seem plausible. You still have to pick an answer though, and if the wrong answer choices are designed to look right, how can you ever be sure that you're not falling for their trap? The best solution we've found to this dilemma is to take the decision out of your hands entirely. Here is the process we recommend:

Once you've eliminated any choices that you are confident (willing to bet $5) are wrong, select the first remaining choice as your answer.

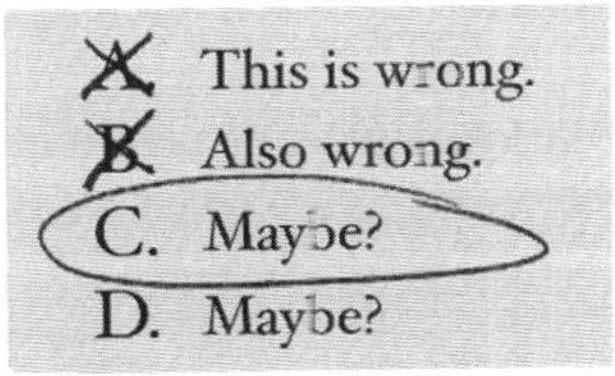

Whether you choose to select the first remaining choice, the second, or the last, the important thing is that you use some preselected standard. Using this approach guarantees that you will not be enticed into selecting an answer choice that looks right, because you are not basing your decision on how the answer choices look.

This is not meant to make you question your knowledge. Instead, it is to help you recognize the difference between your knowledge and your impressions. There's a huge difference between thinking an answer is right because of what you know, and thinking an answer is right because it looks or sounds like it should be right.

Summary: To ensure that your selection is appropriately random, make a predetermined selection from among all answer choices you have not eliminated.

Test-Taking Strategies

This section contains a list of test-taking strategies that you may find helpful as you work through the test. By taking what you know and applying logical thought, you can maximize your chances of answering any question correctly!

It is very important to realize that every question is different and every person is different: no single strategy will work on every question, and no single strategy will work for every person. That's why we've included all of them here, so you can try them out and determine which ones work best for different types of questions and which ones work best for you.

Question Strategies

READ CAREFULLY

Read the question and the answer choices carefully. Don't miss the question because you misread the terms. You have plenty of time to read each question thoroughly and make sure you understand what is being asked. Yet a happy medium must be attained, so don't waste too much time. You must read carefully and efficiently.

CONTEXTUAL CLUES

Look for contextual clues. If the question includes a word you are not familiar with, look at the immediate context for some indication of what the word might mean. Contextual clues can often give you all the information you need to decipher the meaning of an unfamiliar word. Even if you can't determine the meaning, you may be able to narrow down the possibilities enough to make a solid guess at the answer to the question.

PREFIXES

If you're having trouble with a word in the question or answer choices, try dissecting it. Take advantage of every clue that the word might include. Prefixes can be a huge help. Usually, they allow you to determine a basic meaning. *Pre-* means before, *post-* means after, *pro-* is positive, *de-* is negative. From prefixes, you can get an idea of the general meaning of the word and try to put it into context.

HEDGE WORDS

Watch out for critical hedge words, such as *likely, may, can, often, almost, mostly, usually, generally, rarely,* and *sometimes.* Question writers insert these hedge phrases to cover every possibility. Often an answer choice will be wrong simply because it leaves no room for exception. Be on guard for answer choices that have definitive words such as *exactly* and *always.*

SWITCHBACK WORDS

Stay alert for *switchbacks.* These are the words and phrases frequently used to alert you to shifts in thought. The most common switchback words are *but, although,* and *however.* Others include *nevertheless, on the other hand, even though, while, in spite of, despite,* and *regardless of.* Switchback words are important to catch because they can change the direction of the question or an answer choice.

✓ Face Value

When in doubt, use common sense. Accept the situation in the problem at face value. Don't read too much into it. These problems will not require you to make wild assumptions. If you have to go beyond creativity and warp time or space in order to have an answer choice fit the question, then you should move on and consider the other answer choices. These are normal problems rooted in reality. The applicable relationship or explanation may not be readily apparent, but it is there for you to figure out. Use your common sense to interpret anything that isn't clear.

Answer Choice Strategies

✓ Answer Selection

The most thorough way to pick an answer choice is to identify and eliminate wrong answers until only one is left, then confirm it is the correct answer. Sometimes an answer choice may immediately seem right, but be careful. The test writers will usually put more than one reasonable answer choice on each question, so take a second to read all of them and make sure that the other choices are not equally obvious. As long as you have time left, it is better to read every answer choice than to pick the first one that looks right without checking the others.

✓ Answer Choice Families

An answer choice family consists of two (in rare cases, three) answer choices that are very similar in construction and cannot all be true at the same time. If you see two answer choices that are direct opposites or parallels, one of them is usually the correct answer. For instance, if one answer choice says that quantity *x* increases and another either says that quantity *x* decreases (opposite) or says that quantity *y* increases (parallel), then those answer choices would fall into the same family. An answer choice that doesn't match the construction of the answer choice family is more likely to be incorrect. Most questions will not have answer choice families, but when they do appear, you should be prepared to recognize them.

✓ Eliminate Answers

Eliminate answer choices as soon as you realize they are wrong, but make sure you consider all possibilities. If you are eliminating answer choices and realize that the last one you are left with is also wrong, don't panic. Start over and consider each choice again. There may be something you missed the first time that you will realize on the second pass.

✓ Avoid Fact Traps

Don't be distracted by an answer choice that is factually true but doesn't answer the question. You are looking for the choice that answers the question. Stay focused on what the question is asking for so you don't accidentally pick an answer that is true but incorrect. Always go back to the question and make sure the answer choice you've selected actually answers the question and is not merely a true statement.

✓ Extreme Statements

In general, you should avoid answers that put forth extreme actions as standard practice or proclaim controversial ideas as established fact. An answer choice that states the "process should be used in certain situations, if..." is much more likely to be correct than one that states the "process should be discontinued completely." The first is a calm rational statement and doesn't even make a definitive, uncompromising stance, using a hedge word *if* to provide wiggle room, whereas the second choice is far more extreme.

⊘ Benchmark

As you read through the answer choices and you come across one that seems to answer the question well, mentally select that answer choice. This is not your final answer, but it's the one that will help you evaluate the other answer choices. The one that you selected is your benchmark or standard for judging each of the other answer choices. Every other answer choice must be compared to your benchmark. That choice is correct until proven otherwise by another answer choice beating it. If you find a better answer, then that one becomes your new benchmark. Once you've decided that no other choice answers the question as well as your benchmark, you have your final answer.

⊘ Predict the Answer

Before you even start looking at the answer choices, it is often best to try to predict the answer. When you come up with the answer on your own, it is easier to avoid distractions and traps because you will know exactly what to look for. The right answer choice is unlikely to be word-for-word what you came up with, but it should be a close match. Even if you are confident that you have the right answer, you should still take the time to read each option before moving on.

General Strategies

⊘ Tough Questions

If you are stumped on a problem or it appears too hard or too difficult, don't waste time. Move on! Remember though, if you can quickly check for obviously incorrect answer choices, your chances of guessing correctly are greatly improved. Before you completely give up, at least try to knock out a couple of possible answers. Eliminate what you can and then guess at the remaining answer choices before moving on.

⊘ Check Your Work

Since you will probably not know every term listed and the answer to every question, it is important that you get credit for the ones that you do know. Don't miss any questions through careless mistakes. If at all possible, try to take a second to look back over your answer selection and make sure you've selected the correct answer choice and haven't made a costly careless mistake (such as marking an answer choice that you didn't mean to mark). This quick double check should more than pay for itself in caught mistakes for the time it costs.

⊘ Pace Yourself

It's easy to be overwhelmed when you're looking at a page full of questions; your mind is confused and full of random thoughts, and the clock is ticking down faster than you would like. Calm down and maintain the pace that you have set for yourself. Especially as you get down to the last few minutes of the test, don't let the small numbers on the clock make you panic. As long as you are on track by monitoring your pace, you are guaranteed to have time for each question.

⊘ Don't Rush

It is very easy to make errors when you are in a hurry. Maintaining a fast pace in answering questions is pointless if it makes you miss questions that you would have gotten right otherwise. Test writers like to include distracting information and wrong answers that seem right. Taking a little extra time to avoid careless mistakes can make all the difference in your test score. Find a pace that allows you to be confident in the answers that you select.

⊘ Keep Moving

Panicking will not help you pass the test, so do your best to stay calm and keep moving. Taking deep breaths and going through the answer elimination steps you practiced can help to break through a stress barrier and keep your pace.

Final Notes

The combination of a solid foundation of content knowledge and the confidence that comes from practicing your plan for applying that knowledge is the key to maximizing your performance on test day. As your foundation of content knowledge is built up and strengthened, you'll find that the strategies included in this chapter become more and more effective in helping you quickly sift through the distractions and traps of the test to isolate the correct answer.

Now that you're preparing to move forward into the test content chapters of this book, be sure to keep your goal in mind. As you read, think about how you will be able to apply this information on the test. If you've already seen sample questions for the test and you have an idea of the question format and style, try to come up with questions of your own that you can answer based on what you're reading. This will give you valuable practice applying your knowledge in the same ways you can expect to on test day.

Good luck and good studying!

Reading

Literature

Explicit Information

Explicit information is the information stated in a passage or story. It includes facts and statements about the characters in a story as well as about the setting and the events that take place in the story. Explicit information is not merely hinted at; instead, this kind of information is definite, which does not require the reader to draw a conclusion. Explicit information may be found in many forms. It can be in a description, such as "Nora had blue eyes," or in the dialogue "I am from New York City." It also can be found in the actions that characters take. Often this kind of information can be used to support an inference.

Read the following excerpt and identify the explicit information.

> Listen and you will hear the tale of Odin. Odin lived many years ago. He was the head of the gods in what is now Norway. These gods lived in a place called Midgard, and they had many adventures.

Explicit information is information found right within the text, itself. Since explicit information is stated directly in the text, it is not inferred or suggested in any way. The excerpt tells about a god named Odin, who was the head of the gods. They lived in what is now Norway, in a place called Midgard. This information is all explicit, since the passage states it directly. The reader does not need to infer or guess at anything, and nothing is hinted or suggested. Everything is factual, and the reader need not draw a conclusion from the information. When you read, think about the information in the story and whether the information is explicit or not explicit.

Inference

An inference is a conclusion a reader can make from the explicit information found in a passage or story. In addition, an inference often is based on personal experience combined with the information in a passage. For instance, a story may say that a character hears a siren and sees smoke in the distance. From the explicit information in the story and from his or her personal knowledge, the reader can make the logical conclusion that a fire truck is going to a fire. A good inference is supported by the information in a passage. Inferences are not like explicit information, which the passage clearly states. Inferences are not stated in a passage. Instead, the passage hints at inferences. A good reader must put the information together to produce a logical conclusion that is most likely true.

Read the following excerpt and decide why Bonnie liked sailing.

> Bonnie's job was very stressful. She was responsible for looking after several big accounts, and often her phone never stopped ringing. At home at night she would wake up and worry. Watching TV didn't help. But when she was in a boat, with the wind in her face, she forgot all about her job. She could relax.

From this passage, the reader can conclude that Bonnie liked sailing because being in a boat made her feel better. She could relax. The excerpt does not say explicitly that Bonnie liked sailing for these reasons. The reader, however, can infer these reasons for why Bonnie likes sailing. Since sailing made Bonnie relax, it is a "best guess" that Bonnie likes sailing. This is a logical conclusion to the information in the passage, and it is the best conclusion based on what a reader might know from personal experience. An inference is based on the information in a passage and a reader's experience, but it is not stated in the text.

DISCOVERING THE THEME OF A STORY

The theme of a story is the lesson that it teaches, or the moral or what the reader learns from the story. Some themes are used and reused. These themes are called universal themes, and they are related to life, society, human nature, and common situations that arise. Some universal themes include man vs. man or man vs. nature. Other similar themes are "Goodness is rewarded," or "Life evens out." Themes are an important aspect of literature since it teaches the reader or listener a truth about life. The theme is developed by the story's plot and how a character or characters respond to situations in the story.

TELL WHY THE THEME OF THE EXCERPT SHOULD BE "OVERCONFIDENCE BRINGS A FALL."

> One day Conrad bet his friend Billy that he could beat him running, so they had a contest. Billy knew he wasn't very fast, but he kept going. Conrad, who was very fast, started off quickly, but then he stopped to talk to people. Billy passed Conrad by the side of the road and won.

The excerpt tells the story of a boy who bet he could beat his friend in a race. Conrad was faster than Billy, but Billy ended up winning the race. Billy kept going, while Conrad was so confident of the win that he stopped to talk to some people. The story's main point teaches a lesson. If you are overly confident you may have a fall. The theme of a story is the lesson it teaches, and in this excerpt the slower runner who keeps going wins over the faster runner. This universal theme is found often in literature. The fable of the Rabbit and Turtle has a similar theme, but a fable states the theme or moral at the end of the story. Other kinds of fiction do not state the theme at the end of the story.

COMPONENTS OF A SUMMARY

A summary of a story has several components. It should include the main ideas of the passage and also the most important details. These details should support the main idea. A summary is not just a general statement about the story, nor is a summary a paraphrase. Paraphrases reword the main idea and give many supporting ideas in greater detail; summaries do not. A summary will not include everything in the story. In order to write an objective summary, you will need to think about what happens in the story. You will need to decide what is the story is mostly about and what details are most important to the main idea. Summaries are useful since they allow a reader to remember the main idea and the most important details.

DEVELOPMENT OF CHARACTERS

Characters are central to a story. Characters' conflicts and problems make a story interesting and complex. With each event of a story, a character reveals himself or herself to the reader. How characters deal with conflict tells a great deal about their character. How they deal with other characters also tells about what they are feeling. Characters and their actions advance the plot because they show the way in which a story is developing. The way in which characters react tells the reader a great deal about their nature. They also help the reader understand the theme or lesson that the story teaches. Characters' ultimate outcome is central to the development of the theme of a story.

EXPLAIN HOW THE TWO CHARACTERS INTERACT WITH EACH OTHER.

> Veronica felt her knees shaking as the gym class began. She looked at the rope stretching up to the ceiling. She took the rope in one hand. She kept thinking what would happen if she fell. Then

> she heard her friend Alice call out, "You can do it, kiddo!" She smiled. Hand over hand; she started to climb up the rope.

In the passage, Veronica feels the conflict of fear or failure. She is worried about climbing the rope. She wonders what will happen if she falls while climbing the rope. The reader does not know why Veronica is afraid, but her shaking knees tell the reader of the tension Veronica is feeling. The setting is the school gym. After her friend Alice calls out words of encouragement, Veronica's demeanor changes and she smiles. Her fear of failure is gone, and she begins to climb the rope. The two characters obviously are close friends, and Alice's words change Veronica and give her strength to challenge the rope. This is how they interact with one another.

EXPLAIN HOW THE CHARACTER IN THE EXCERPT SHAPES THE THEME.

> Norman put his hands on the wheel. He looked at the driving officer who nodded to begin. Norman pulled out. He followed the officer's instructions. Norman wondered if his nervousness showed. He thought about all the lessons he had taken, and how they all led to this point. It seemed like an eternity before he heard the words, "You passed."

The setting is the inside of a car, and the plot revolves around Norman as he begins to take the road test for his driver's license, one of the biggest events in any teenager's life. The conflict revolves around whether he will pass or fail. Norman remembers his Driver's Ed lessons, and the many hours he spent in a car with his teacher. The theme is definitely coming of age. Norman shapes the theme by being lost in concentration and trying not to make a mistake until he hears the words he had hoped for: "You passed." The theme is intertwined with Norman's emotions. He shapes the theme.

CONTEXT CLUES

The best way to figure out the meaning of unknown words and expressions is to examine the surrounding context clues. Often many clues to the meaning of an expression or word in the sentences occur just before or after the unknown word or expression. Some words have more than one meaning, and only through the context of the text can these words be understood. For instance, the word "blunt" has several meanings, including "having a dull edge," "not being subtle," and "being slow to understand," so understanding the context is important. In the sentence, "He was a blunt talker, and I got his point quickly," it becomes clear that the meaning is "not being subtle." Phrases also must be understood through context. In the sentence, "She rolled up her sleeves and got to work," the reader can get the sense that "rolling up her sleeves" means to get ready for hard work.

FIGURATIVE LANGUAGE

Figurative language is the use of words and expressions to expand reality in a vivid way. An author can use language in a non-literal way, which means using language in a non-traditional manner in order to create an image. Examples of figurative language include simile, metaphor, personification, and hyperbole as well as onomatopoeia and alliteration. Similes compare things using the words *like* or *as,* for example, "He is strong as an ox." Metaphors compare things without using comparing words, for example, "He is an ox when it comes to work." Personification gives a thing or animal human traits, for example, "The trees talked to me of days gone by." Hyperbole is an exaggeration that is not believable: "He is the most exciting individual that exists on the planet."Onomatopoeia is when words sound like what they are, "moo, moo"; and alliteration involves using words successively that start with the same letter: "Baa, baa, black sheep...."

READ THE EXCERPT.

> Jim watched with awe as Marianne sliced her way effortlessly through the commuters crowded together in the train station.

TELL WHAT FORM THE PHRASE "SLICED ITS WAY EFFORTLESSLY" IS AND WHY.

The phrase "sliced her way effortlessly" is an example of a figure of speech called a metaphor. Metaphors add depth to writing and make it richer. They are used to create a more vivid image of something in the reader's mind, in this case like a knife easily slicing through something without any resistance, like a piece of cake. This example is not a simile because it doesn't use a word such as "like" to compare two things. It can't be hyperbole, since the phrase is not an exaggeration. This phrase is not an example of personification because Marianne is human.

DENOTATIVE AND CONNOTATIVE MEANINGS OF WORDS

A word can have both a denotative meaning and a connotative meaning. The denotative meaning is the actual meaning of a word. The connotative meaning refers to the associations a word has above and beyond its literal meaning. For instance, the word "frugal" might mean "careful with money" or "economical," while the word "miserly" adds another dimension to the understanding of what someone is like. "Miserly" has a much more negative connotation than does "frugal." When writers describe characters, they often use words with strong connotations to hint at what a character is like, so readers should analyze the writer's choice of words.

READ THE FOLLOWING SENTENCE.

> The boy's friends considered him brilliant, but many others considered him merely shrewd.

DETERMINE HOW THE CONNOTATIVE MEANINGS OF THE WORD "SHREWD" AND HOW IT COMPARES WITH THE WORD "BRILLIANT."

Both the words "shrewd" and "brilliant" have a dictionary (denotative) meaning of "sharply intelligent" or "keenly aware." The word "shrewd," however, also has a connotation of cunning or slyness rather than just intelligence. When compared with the word "brilliant," "shrewd" is negative. It connotes a slipperiness that could be associated with a snake. The connotations a word adds to a sentence influence how the reader grasps the meaning; therefore, readers closely should study the words a writer uses. In this instance, the writer has drawn a contrast between positive and negative.

CLUES TO THE SETTING, CHARACTER, AND EVENTS

The words a writer uses to tell a story are of ultimate importance. They give clues to the setting, character, and events. Many words help evoke a sense of time, place, or the setting in which a story takes place. The words suggest the time of day, the time of year, and whether the action takes place a long time ago or in the future. The words also suggest the place where the action occurs by describing items the character sees, uses, or encounters. A writer's words are like the colors a painter uses. A writer's words build one on the other to give the reader a sense of when and where a story occurs.

DETERMINE HOW THE CHOICE OF WORDS IN THE EXCERPT EVOKES A SENSE OF TIME AND PLACE.

> Isabel walked through the hall covered with paintings of her ancestors. Down the stairs, she went to the ball room. The dim gas light made everything seem mysterious. She lifted her heavy skirts to ensure she would not fall.

Words can evoke many things. Often they evoke a sense of time and place. The words in the excerpt describe a hall covered with paintings and a ball room. Few homes today have ball rooms. The excerpt talks about having gas light, a certain clue to a time in the past. Isabel lifts her heavy skirts, which also evokes the past and a sense of grandeur. These are just a few examples of how language evokes a sense of time and place. When reading, make sure to take in the descriptions and hints the writer gives about the time and place in which the story occurs.

READ THE FOLLOWING EXCERPT.

> I went to this railroad museum yesterday. It was way cool. I didn't want to leave. I saw loads of model trains. They were running in all sorts of directions. They had hills and tunnels. The streets even had little people.

DETERMINE HOW THE PASSAGE IS AN EXAMPLE OF AN INFORMAL TONE.

The two main styles of writing are formal writing and informal writing. This excerpt is an example of an informal tone, because it makes use of short sentences instead of the longer more complex sentences found in formal writing. The excerpt uses the more casual first person rather than the third person viewpoint, usually used in formal writing. The writer also makes use of colloquial expressions such as "way cool," which formal writers avoid. Another sign of the informal tone is the writer's use of the contraction, "didn't." Formal writing avoids the use of contractions. The expression "loads of" is considered a cliché. Clichés are often used in informal writing, but they are not used in formal style.

PARALLEL PLOTS

Many stories feature parallel plots, or stories within stories, with more than one conflict and more than one main character. These plots are usually related to one another and often add a sense of greater depth than a story with a single plot. While for the most part, short stories are focused on one plot, multiple plots usually are found in novels, most notably in long novels. Some of the most notable examples of parallel plots are found in foreign language books. Russian novels are known for their numerous parallel plots and large numbers of characters Parallel plots often give a novel a sense of family and history that cannot exist in stories revolving only around one plot.

FLASHBACKS

Flashbacks are a frequently used device especially in movies, but also in short stories and novels. A flashback is a view of something that will happen in the future, and it occurs out of sequence in regard to the chronology of the story's events. For these reasons, flashbacks can have strong effects on literature. They hint at what is to come, and they give the audience or reader an inkling of what might happen. As a result, they easily can create a sense of mystery, tension, or surprise. Generally a story only features one flashback, which often occurs at the beginning of the story. It often sets the stage for conflict that will arise in the narrative. A flashback is one kind of literary device writers use for effect.

PACING

The pacing of a story is its rhythm, which is unique to every story. The pacing is the rate at which a story unfolds or is told. Accordingly, sometimes a story's pacing is slow and leisurely, while at other times it is rapid fire. Writers try to match the pacing of a story with kind of story being told and the characters in the story. A story may start out very slowly and then speed up to a racing rate. The pacing is the heart of a story, and a writer must feel her or his way with it. Variety of pacing is important because it can draw the reader into what is happening. Too much pacing at the same level could become boring. Pacing is the means a writer uses to involve the reader in what happens in the story.

Analyzing Literature from Outside the US

Literature from outside the United States, by its very nature, will contain many different points of views and cultural experiences from those contained in American literature. Characters in books written by people other than Americans may reflect their writers' cultures rather than American culture. As a result, sometimes figuring out exactly what is happening or what an author is attempting to say in a story can prove difficult without some basic knowledge of the writer's culture. One way to discover different viewpoints is to study in what ways a foreign book is different. For instance, Latin American literature often contains references to more cultural turmoil than exists in the United States. Russian literature often infuses a sense of hopelessness into the story, as is the case in Anton Chekov, the great Russian playwright. Characters in Chekov's dramas often face insurmountable problems. Asian literature has a different sense of the importance of the individual than does American literature, as well as a greater sense of respect for tradition and family than is common in American literature.

Discover the cultural differences expressed in the excerpt.

> The three brothers walked through the jungle to a clearing, where they saw a house. They were hungry and tired. They knew the owner was obliged to feed them and let them stay the night, so they knocked at the door.

Many cultural differences in this excerpt affect the story. First, the brothers are walking through the jungle, an experience not part of everyday life in the United States. Also, this passage refers to the house owner's obligation to feed the brothers and invite them to stay the night. These actions represent very different customs than those readily expressed in the United States. As such, a reader might better understand the story if he or she realizes that oftentimes in other countries, people do not have hotels or places to stay other than a person's home. Without this knowledge, the reader may have difficulty comprehending the lesson the writer is trying to teach.

Determine the difference between the way Peter Breughel's Landscape with the Fall of Icarus and W. H. Auden's "Musée des Beaux Arts" interpret and represent the same subject

The legend of Icarus tells the story of a young man whose father, Daedalus, an inventor, creates wings for Icarus and for himself. He fastens the wings to his son with wax so they can escape from their prison. He then cautions Icarus not to fly too close to the sun because the wax will melt. Icarus does not obey his father, and he falls from the sky. Breughel's painting depicts the scene of Icarus' fall, in which no one is interested enough to stop to observe the tragic death of Icarus. Auden, a poet, saw the painting in the museum mentioned in the poem's title, and in the poem he comments on the apathy people show towards suffering. Breughel's painting is a silent representation of the apathy which Auden verbalizes.

Ways Universal Themes Are Impacted by the Time in Which They Were Written

While universal themes are the same in terms of their meaning and the topics they depict or teach, their presentations are affected by the time in which a literary piece is written. The characters and situations portrayed will mirror the environment in which the writer lived. Ancient literature depicts a time when myth was alive and when the concept of personal freedom still was evolving and not taken for granted. Many Greek plays employ universal themes.

Explain the similarities present in the themes found in "Metamorphoses" by the Latin poet Ovid and the play As You Like It by British playwright William Shakespeare.

"Metamorphoses," which means transformations or changes, is an epic poem written by Ovid. It details the ways in which nymphs and people are transformed into plants and animals and how springs appear from nowhere. Shakespeare's comedy addresses a similar theme, namely the way in which people change, although the Shakespearean characters undergo mental changes rather than physical changes. When Shakespeare's characters enter Arden, they practically assume new identities that ultimately allow them to change and grow as people. Both works also address the affect of love on humans and natural human theatrics expressed through song.

Explain how the musical West Side Story relates to the Shakespearean play Romeo and Juliet.

William Shakespeare's tragedy Romeo and Juliet tells the story of a young man and young woman who fall in love, even though their parents are enemies of one another. This play is a tragedy because the young couple dies at the play's conclusion when they fall victim to their parents' warring. The play utilizes dialogue that by today's standards sounds dated and sometimes difficult to understand. The musical *West Side Story* is also about two young people from different cultural backgrounds who fall in love and then die victims of the hatred between Hispanics and Italian-Americans in a poor section of New York City. In the musical, songs and lyrics develop the plot, unlike in Shakespeare's play. The language is modern and the action takes place in a modern world, but the themes are precisely the same.

Explain why the ability to read and comprehend a wide-variety of texts by the end of grade 10 is vital.

A student should be able to comprehend a wide variety of texts by the end of tenth grade for many reasons. This background will give the student a great advantage to achieve success in school, especially in the next two years of high school and then college, if this is a goal. Being able to read a wide number of different texts will reward the student with greater knowledge of the world and a growing awareness of cultural differences. In addition, reading has the extra benefit of helping students develop their vocabulary. Ultimately, reading a large number of different literary books will educate the student in many fields and is an excellent preparation for life in general.

Informational text

Finding textual evidence

Explicit information is information stated in a text rather than merely hinted at in the text. A nonfiction text typically makes various statements or claims based on supporting details. These statements or claims are explicit, and as such, supporting details need to present accurate evidence. When trying to find textual evidence for explicit material in a text, the reader should look for details that tell about the explicit information and give more information. The supporting information should be based on fact, not opinion. Furthermore, the supporting information should come from a reliable source and be verifiable.

Inference

An inference is a best guess, or the conclusion the reader can make from information in the passage. For instance, if a passage cites studies showing that teenagers need eight hours of sleep per night to do well in school, but also tells how getting to school early interferes with teenagers getting enough sleep, the reader might conclude that teenagers often are tired. While the text does not make this as a direct statement, the reader can figure it out. While the conclusion might be wrong, the reader likely can make the connection as a best guess. When you make an inference, you need to be able to cite the textual evidence upon which the inference is based. In this case, the fact that teenagers are not getting as much sleep as they need because they have to get to school early leads the reader to conclude that teenagers often are tired.

IDENTIFY WHICH INFORMATION IN THE EXCERPT SUPPORTS THE INFERENCE THAT SUGAR CANE NEEDS A HOTTER CLIMATE THAN SUGAR BEETS.

> Sugar cane resembles a tall grass; it needs hot sun and rain to thrive. The cane fills with a dark green juice. Sugar is made from the juice. Sugar beets do not need a lot of heat or rain. The sugar also is made from juice from the beets.

The passage states that sugar cane needs hot sun and rain to thrive supports the inference that sugar cane needs a hotter climate in which to grow than do sugar beets. Another supporting detail is that sugar beets do not need a lot of heat or rain to grow. Since the excerpt states as such, this explicit evidence supports the inference or conclusion. The other details explain the process of obtaining the juice from the two plants, which is then made into sugar, but they do not give details about the right climate for the plants. An inference is the best conclusion a reader can make based on the information given.

DETERMINING THE CENTRAL IDEA OF A PASSAGE

The central idea of a passage is what the passage is mostly about. It is the main point of the passage. Sometimes a passage states the main idea. In such passages, the main idea can be found in a topic sentence at the beginning of the passage or somewhere in the text. Sometimes the main idea is found in the conclusion of a passage. Oftentimes, however, the passage does not state the main idea outright. Instead, the reader needs to figure it out from the information or supporting details found in the passage. The main idea will become more and more evident as a person reads a passage. Most of the time, the main idea does not become evident until the reader has reached nearly the end of the passage. The central or main idea becomes evident as the reader encounters more details and information about the main idea. The details shape the main idea.

DISCUSS WHY THE MAIN IDEA OF THIS EXCERPT IS "THE IRISH HAVE A LONG HISTORY."

> The Irish people of today descended from the three sons of Milesius, the king of Hispania, now known as Spain. They invaded Ireland a thousand years before Christ and intermarried with the local natives, known as the Tuatha De Danaan, who are said to have descended from the Irish goddess Danu.

The information in the excerpt deals the descendants of the Irish people. Furthermore, the passage tells how the three sons of the king of what is now Spain invaded Ireland and married the local natives. The details about the Irish are explicit, accurate facts and can be checked. The central idea emerges from these details. The details tell the early history of the Irish people. Supporting details shape or tell more about the main idea so the reader can tell what a passage is mostly about.

COMPONENTS OF A SUMMARY

A summary of an informational text tells what the text is about and includes some details. It should include the main idea of the passage and the most important supporting details. A summary should be to the point, but also it should include important facts, events, or evidence telling why the text is important or why it was written. Make sure a summary is objective by focusing on the main idea rather than any statements unrelated to the text's main idea. Unlike paraphrasing, a summary is not lengthy and does not include all of the details. It focuses on the most important supporting information to the main idea.

ANALYZING THE AUTHOR'S GOALS AND IDEAS

Every author writes differently, and every type of nonfiction passage has a different goal. The reader's job is to determine the way the author has chosen to present his or her goals and ideas. When you read, you need to ask yourself whether the ideas are presented in a logical, rhetorical, or persuasive manner. You need to seek to discover the author's goal and analyze the way in which the author makes his or her points. You also need to analyze whether the points an author makes seem valid by looking for supporting evidence or reliable and based on fact rather than on opinion.

Connecting the Ideas in a Nonfiction Passage

Not only do nonfiction passages have main ideas, but they also have details. Oftentimes these details are supporting details. The reader's job is to understand how these details relate to one another and to the main idea. A careful reader will analyze the author's intent and then consider the author's ideas to see where they lead. The connected ideas form a trail through the text leading to the conclusion. Readers should evaluate the ideas individually to see if they are sound and based on fact rather than opinion. Connecting ideas is the essence of a nonfiction passage.

Context Clues

Oftentimes the meaning of unknown words and phrases can be grasped from the context of the sentence in which they are used or from the sentences immediately before or after the unknown words or phrases. Occasionally, in the case of a technical document, reading the entire passage may be necessary in order to understand the meaning of certain technical terms. Words and phrases used in a figurative manner rather than in a literal manner can be difficult to understand without understanding the context of an entire passage. Idioms also can prove difficult to understand and need to be studied in terms of the context of the text for comprehension.

Determine the kind of language and tone used in the following court ruling.

> "... the prosecution may not use statements, whether exculpatory or inculpatory, stemming from custodial interrogation of the defendant unless it demonstrates the use of procedural safeguards effective to secure the privilege against self-incrimination." (Miranda v. Arizona, 1966)

The language in the court ruling is very formal and technical. It relies on many words drawn from Latin roots, a common language used by lawyers in the courtroom. The key words "exculpatory" and "inculpatory" both derive from the Latin root word "culpa," which means "blame." The prefix "ex-" means "out of" while the prefix "in-" means the opposite. The words mean "cleared of blame" and "blamed" or "incriminated." "Interrogation" also comes from a Latin word meaning "asking" and is defined as "examination by official questioning." "Custodial" is the adjective form of "custody" and means "related to the work of guarding." The word "incrimination" contains the simpler word "crime" and points to the meaning "to cause to appear guilty." The affect of such language makes the court ruling extremely formal and technical.

Determine the language and tone of this newspaper article.

> American Neil Armstrong has become the first man to walk on the Moon.
>
> The astronaut stepped onto the Moon's surface...after first opening the hatch on the Eagle landing craft.
>
> As he put his left foot down first Armstrong declared: "That's one small step for man, one giant leap for mankind."

The excerpt, written July 21, 1969, by the BBC after the Apollo 11 Mission landed on the surface of the moon, shares several attributes with common journalistic language. Paragraphs are short, usually just one or two sentences. The most important facts come first. The basic questions: who, what, when, where and why form the core of the writing. Information is exact. Quotation marks are used in exact wording. The language is easy to comprehend, avoiding any words that the average reader would find difficult to understand. The tone is factual and objective, without any opinion.

READ THE FOLLOWING EXCERPT AND EXPLAIN ITS MEANING.

> To qualify for Social Security disability benefits, first you must have worked in jobs covered by Social Security. Next, you must have a medical condition that meets Social Security's definition of disability. In general, we pay monthly cash benefits to people who are unable to work for a year or more because of a disability.

The passage covers the two criteria necessary to obtain disability benefits from the Social Security Administration. First, you must have worked in a job and paid social security taxes. It is inferred, therefore, that some jobs are not eligible. Secondly, the information states that your medical condition must be one that Social Security covers, so, again, some medical conditions might be ineligible. Once you have satisfied the two conditions, then you will begin receiving money on a monthly basis from Social Security. However, the information also says you have to have been out of work because of disability for at least a year. In order to understand the excerpt, you would have to understand some of the technical language. You would have to figure out what *disability* means. You would have to figure out what is meant by *medical condition*. Another technical expression is *cash benefits.*

FIGURATIVE LANGUAGE.

Figurative language is the use of ordinary language in a non-literal way or non-traditional manner. A writer uses figurative language to expand his or her vision by interjecting images into their writing to make it more colorful and fresh. The literal meaning of a word or phrase is bypassed and a non-literal meaning is attached to it. Further, various kinds of figurative language exist. A simile compares two things using the words *as* or *like.* For example, "His heart was as good as gold." A metaphor compares two things without using the comparing words: "He had a heart of gold." Personification gives a thing or animal human traits, for example, "His heart spoke to me." When reading, look for non-traditional ways of using language for hints to the meaning of the passage.

WHAT KIND OF FIGURATIVE LANGUAGE DOES THIS EXCERPT USE?

> Samantha often thought her kid brother had a brain the size of a pea.

This is an example of a figure of speech called a hyperbole or an exaggeration. This figure of speech is used to create an effect on the reader or to make a point. In this case the wording emphasizes that she thought her kid brother was really dumb and must have a tiny brain. Hyperboles often add a touch of humor to writing and can be found in everyday writing as well as in fiction and poetry. Such language is not meant to be taken literally. This extreme exaggeration differentiates a hyperbole from a metaphor. This example is not personification because it does not attach a human characteristic to an object or an animal.

DENOTATIVE AND CONNOTATIVE MEANINGS OF WORDS

The denotative meaning of a word is the literal definition of a word that often can be found in a dictionary. The connotative meaning is somewhat more subtle; it may also be listed in a dictionary, but this listing will occur after the literal meaning. The connotative meaning is suggested by the word. It is not stated outright, but its usage has established its more hidden meaning. For instance, the words "hefty" and "obese" both mean fat, but obese has the connotation of being unhealthily fat, while hefty is a gentler description and means somewhat fatter than usual. When reading texts, it is a good idea to notice any words with strong connotations, since these words are a key to the author's opinion or point of view.

READ THE FOLLOWING.

Her mother told her she was too skinny, but Jennifer always felt that she was really slender.

EXPLAIN THE CONNOTATIVE MEANINGS OF THE WORD "SKINNY" AND HOW IT COMPARES WITH THE WORD "SLENDER."

Both the words "skinny" and "slender" can be defined as "thin" or "lean." The word "skinny" has a certain air of unattractiveness about it, while the word "slender" connotes gracefulness, even an air of stylish vogue, so Jennifer and her mother definitely have a different viewpoint. When writing, choose words carefully so you don't depict something in a negative way, when you really mean to depict it in a positive light. Utilize the dictionary for help when choosing words. Furthermore, the thesaurus is useful for listing different connotations of synonyms. By following these suggestions, your words will project exactly what you want to say to your readers. In the same way, check a text for words that have negative or positive connotations. These words are a clue to what a writer thinks about a person or situation.

HOW AN AUTHOR'S IDEAS OR CLAIMS CAN BE DEVELOPED AND REFINED

When authors write a passage, they choose from a variety of ways to bring the reader their ideas or claims. The author must decide how best to present and develop the material and ideas, sometimes including creating sentences, paragraphs, or even larger portions of a text dedicated to the development of one idea. A complicated idea may require a large segment of a text, while some simple ideas could be explained in a single sentence. Oftentimes authors will use subheads to create a clearer focus for the reader to look quickly look through the subheads and determine the location of information. This method way of organizing allows the author to explain several different topics in one passage and helps organize the material as well. When reading, look at the ways in which the author structures his or her ideas.

DETERMINE WHY IT WOULD BE USEFUL FOR HER TO USE SUBHEADS.

Leslie is working on a report on the destruction of the rainforests. She wants to include information on various aspects of why the destruction is happening and the effect of such destruction on nature and wildlife.

Subheads are an excellent way to organize material and provide the reader with a quick idea of the passage's main content. In a nonfiction passage, often many ideas need to be explored, explained, and developed. To keep them from competing with one another and to keep a reader from becoming confused, subheads can help organize a lot of information that could be lost if lumped under one broad title. Subheads also allow a writer to deviate slightly from the overall main idea so the writer can explain in more depth about one aspect of a topic.

DETERMINING AN AUTHOR'S POINT OF VIEW

The author's point of view is not always immediately evident. Although stated clearly in many texts, often the main point of view is hidden. In such situations, the reader needs to discover through attention to the author's word choice. It is important to read a text closely to figure out what an author thinks about an event, person, topic or issue. When reading, always check for any emotional statements that give hints about the author's feelings. Some authors make their opinions and viewpoints clear when they embrace the use of rhetoric. Rhetoric is effective speaking and persuasion through the use of strong and fresh language meant to sway an audience. Rhetoric can be effective, and the reader may not be aware of how much it is influencing him or her. For this reason, readers should analyze texts for persuasive techniques. A reader needs to know the author's viewpoint before the reader can decide on her or his own.

DISCUSS THE PURPOSE OF RHETORIC IN THE FOLLOWING PASSAGE.

> "He that would make his own liberty secure, must guard even his enemy from oppression; for if he violates this duty, he establishes a precedent which will reach to himself." Thomas Paine, 1795

The excerpt, written by Thomas Paine, one of the Founding Fathers of the United States, uses rhetoric to advance his argument that one sometimes must do what does not come naturally, i.e. protect your enemy, or you yourself may one day be in danger. This passage is meant to make the reader think about liberty. Rhetoric is an oratorical device and a means of persuading an audience. Rhetoric is applicable to both logic and politics. It uses language to create an effect, and it also uses that language to create a more lasting image that is easily recalled afterwards. Rhetoric uses words to motivate actions by others.

DETAILS OF A PERSON'S LIFE MIGHT BE EMPHASIZED IN A MOVIE THAT WOULD NOT BE EMPHASIZED AS MUCH IN A WRITTEN BIOGRAPHY

A movie is a visual medium; a book is a written medium. A person's life would be visualized in a movie in a way it could not be visualized in a book. Primarily, the person playing the subject would act in a certain way that might not be discussed in a written account. For instance, the way a person wears her or his hair, or the way a person walks and talks are not details that a book could describe as successfully. Other details that would be more evident in a movie version of someone's life are the small reactions to events or people that might be omitted from a written account. Much difference exists between the two media; the movie would tend to be more dramatic than the book, as well.

EVIDENCE BASED CLAIMS

Authors often make claims, but it is important that these claims are backed with evidence. This evidence, however, must come from valid sources in order to be accepted. Sources include books written by experts on a subject, information from accredited studies, and trustworthy Internet sources. When analyzing a source, ask yourself if evidence exists asserting the source as an authority on the subject at hand. When reviewing an author's statements, see if reliable sources for the statements exist. If no such information exists, the statements probably are fallacious.

DISCUSS HOW THE EXCERPT BELOW RELATES TO A COMMON AMERICAN THEME.

> "...Oppressed people cannot remain oppressed forever. The yearning for freedom eventually manifests itself, and that is what has happened to the American Negro. Something within has reminded him of his birthright of freedom, and something without has reminded him that it can be gained. Consciously or unconsciously, he has been caught up by the Zeitgeist..."

This excerpt is taken from Martin Luther King, Jr.'s, *Letter from Birmingham Jail,* 1963. Arrested for taking part in a non-violent protest against racial injustice, King wrote the letter to affirm his belief only non-violent protest would help African Americans achieve civil rights. It immediately had a significant impact by starting a dialogue between blacks and whites. The theme of freedom for all people has been the bedrock of American political thought since the country's founding. Civil disobedience was justified, according to Dr. King, because the existing laws were unjust. "Zeitgeist" means "spirit of the times" in German, and refers to the cultural, ethical, and political climate is prevalent at the time.

Explain why becoming a proficient reader of literary nonfiction texts by grade 10 is important.

By the end of grade 10, a student should be able to read nonfiction proficiently because this skill will enable the student to excel in the last two years of high school. Furthermore, by the end of grade 10, students are becoming more independent, taking on jobs, and relating to people and situations independently, so they need to be able to comprehend all kinds of written passages. Without the ability to comprehend material he or she reads, a student will fall behind and develop unfortunate habits of reading without comprehension. Good reading abilities will carry the student through high school to a working position or a college campus. However, without these skills, the student is handicapped.

Writing

PRODUCING CLEAR AND COHERENT WRITING

Each genre of writing requires its own traits, but to attain clear and coherent writing it is necessary to plan what you will be writing. First, decide on your goal, or whether you are trying to inform, persuade, or entertain. With your goal in mind, you need to organize your material if you are writing a nonfiction piece. You need to have a clear idea of your main ideas and supporting details. If you are planning to write a narrative, you need to pay attention to developing your story in a clear and flowing manner. Then, create characters through skillful use of description, dialogue, and action. In addition in all types of writing you need to establish a tone. You also need to make sure your writing is free of grammatical or spelling errors. Close rereading and editing is part of the writing process, as well.

IMPORTANCE OF PLANNING, REVISING, EDITING, AND REVIEWING A TEXT TO MAKE IT REACH A SPECIFIC AUDIENCE

When beginning to write, you should develop a plan about what you want to discuss and the points you want to make. An outline can prove helpful if you are writing a nonfiction piece. If you are writing a narrative, you might want to make a story map. Next, you should write a first draft. Once you have finished the writing, you should put it aside for a time. When you come back to it, you will see it with fresh eyes and will see more easily what needs to be changed or revised. After you make the revisions and put the writing aside again, then reread the writing and begin to edit it for any grammatical, spelling, punctuation, or usage errors. Make sure that the supporting details are clear and in a logical order in a report. Rework the dialogue to make it more precise in a story. Read your work to someone else and ask for feedback. Finally, revise it again.

READ THE FOLLOWING PASSAGE, EXPLAIN WHY IT NEEDS REVISION, AND TELL HOW TO REVISE IT.

> Learning how to play lacrosse is too hard. Everyone knows lacrosse was invented by the Indians. But let me tell you it is a cool game. It's played with a stick that hits a ball that goes into an opponent's net for a goal. And it move's fast.

The writer of the passage has not made clear what she is trying to communicate. The passage is unorganized, and it contains grammatical errors, usage errors, and clichés.

HERE IS A REVISION THAT READS MUCH BETTER:

> Lacrosse, a sport originated by Native Americans, is a fast-moving game played with a lacrosse stick and a small, hard rubber ball. The object of the game is to use the stick to get the ball into the opponent's net and score a goal. It is not an easy game, but it is enjoyable.

Here, the writer has organized her thoughts in a logical order. The writing has a definite statement (*lacrosse is a fast-moving game)* and tells about the object of the game (*get the ball into the opponent's net).* It also includes the writer's feelings about the game as a conclusion. Everything now makes sense and the passage is free of grammatical and usage errors.

USING THE INTERNET

Online sources are a wonderful tool for writers. They can get works published at little or no cost either as an e-book or a printed book. There are other options available as well, such as editing and marketing services offered on many Internet sites. Writing tools give help with everything from style to grammar. Many sites are reliable research possibilities and provide accurate and objective information. Make sure to pick reliable sources for any research. Also, be sure to cite Internet sources using an accepted format such as that from the MLA (Modern Language Association). Many sites allow people to work together on projects regardless of their physical location. Chat rooms and topic websites are other tools that allow exchanges of information and have shared writing projects.

CONDUCTING A SHORT RESEARCH PROJECT

A plan of action is a good first step when conducting a short or a sustained research project to answer a question or solve a problem. Before you go online, make a list of key words relating to the question or problem. Utilize these words either in a search engine or an online or print encyclopedia. You can consult many sources to find the information you are seeking. Back issues of magazines, journals, and newspapers also can be of use. Meet your objective by finding an answer to a question or a solution to a problem. Use information from many sources and then synthesize it so the writing flows logically. Show that you have a good grasp of the subject and what it encompasses.

Make an outline including the kind of information you are seeking as well as the scope of the project. Then make a list of pertinent keywords to search for the topic in multiple print and digital sources. Take notes and make an outline of the similarities as well as the differences you encounter in various sources. Journals, text books, magazines, and newspapers are of use; the number of sources you can uncover is limitless. Whatever the source, verify its timeliness, accuracy, and credibility. Dismiss any sources that seem questionable. When recording the information, make sure to use fresh language and not copy anything directly except for quotations cited appropriately to avoid plagiarism. Use the Modern Language Association (MLA) guidelines for all citations.

ANALYZE HOW TOM STOPPARD USED A SHAKESPEAREAN PLAY FOR THE BASIS OF HIS PLAY ROSENKRANTZ & GUILDENSTERN ARE DEAD.

Stoppard's play *Rosenkrantz & Guildenstern Are Dead* is a mirror image of Shakespeare's *Hamlet*. In Stoppard's play, Rosenkrantz and Guildenstern are the main characters. They portray schoolmates who wander around aimlessly, bewildered by the events that take place around them, and babble nonsense to each other. In *Hamlet,* the two never appeared on stage. In Stoppard's play, these characters come across a theatrical troupe called the Tragedians and find themselves in a performance of *Hamlet*. They are asked to help Prince Hamlet, who may or may not be going insane. The play depicts a searching for values and dismay that nothing is certain. As one character called The Player says, "Uncertainty is the normal state. You're nobody special." Unlike Hamlet, this play is written in modern language, but the two works have similar themes.

JERRY IS WRITING AN ARTICLE ABOUT SPACE TRAVEL. EVALUATE THE FOLLOWING SOURCES AS TO THEIR RELIABILITY..

http://www.nasa.gov/home/index.html

Encyclopedia Britannica, 15th edition, © 1986

When doing research, information gathered from print sources often can be just as reliable as information obtained from the Internet. However, when researching space travel, the information included in the Encyclopedia Britannica would be too dated and would be missing important information from 1986 until now. Such an encyclopedia would be reliable if you were researching classical Greek philosophy. For research on space travel, though, the NASA (National Aeronautics and Space Administration) website would be much more reliable and up-to-date. For these reasons, it is important always to check the date on all sources to make sure they contain the latest information so your research will not be outdated.

Writing Routinely

Students should learn to write routinely. Whatever the task or purpose, students need to be able to put their ideas into words. There are various types of writing. A report may take longer to write than a short answer to a question. Students need to learn to pace themselves when writing longer pieces. They should be prepared to write a rough draft and then revise, edit, and revise again. Shorter writing assignments will not require as much attention since their structure is more straight forward. Nonetheless, whether writing short or long pieces, students need to find a way to become communicators with the written word, including employing proper grammar, spelling, and varied syntax in order to keep the reader interested.

Persuasive text

Introducing a Claim

An excellent way to introduce an argument in a persuasive passage and create an appropriate organization involves ordering your claims and then finding research that supports those claims. A good way to begin is making an outline. Put your claim at the top, and then list the reasons and the evidence supporting the statement. This can be done if you have more than one claim. Include counterclaims and evidence of why you do not think they are correct. When you write the passage, hold the reader's attention by using a strong tone, rhetoric, and fresh language. Be sure to your claims with evidence from acceptable sources. Finally, restating your mail claim at the conclusion of your passage is a good idea.

Providing the Most Relevant Evidence

Whether presenting a claim or a counterclaim, you should include supporting evidence for each one. Even though you are emphasizing your claim, you still need to include reliable information about the counterclaim. Including this information will increase the effectiveness of your argument by presenting both sides. The evidence needs to be reliable and relevant and should cover every point made. You need to do a great deal of research to develop your evidence. While researching, try to anticipate what readers might say; this anticipation will help you develop your claim thoroughly. It is not enough to research a claim on the Internet because many internet sources are dubious at best. Instead, look for objective sites. Find experts that you can quote, and use proven statistics. Give each claim and counterclaim its own paragraph or two. Make sure to present your information in a logical manner so the reader easily can understand.

Creating Cohesion

The best way to create cohesion between claims and evidence is to organize your ideas and then write sentences explaining your reasons and providing evidence that follows your main ideas logically. Careful research will make your argument cohesive and easy to understand. Your claim and evidence should relate clearly to each other. Words indicating to the reader that the claim and evidence are related include: *since, because, as a consequence* or *as a result.* You also can utilize clauses to demonstrate a relationship between the reason and the effect. *As a result of Dr. Long's experiment, more and more people have come to the realization that this new product is flawed.* The first clause sets the tone and establishes causality between the reason and effect. After writing, re-read to verify that relationships between cause and effect are logical.

Maintaining a Formal Style

A formal style is the usual style when writing arguments. This style helps the writer achieve objectivity and keeps the language precise. Formal writing consists of complete sentences; fragments should be avoided unless used for a specific reason. Do not use the first or second person. The third person is standard in formal writing. Use an active voice, which projects more energy, and avoid the passive voice. Do not use contractions and make sure not to change tenses between sentences or paragraphs. Ensure that you use proper spelling and punctuation. Reread and edit your passage several times to improve the language wherever possible. Make sure your ideas follow a logical order, as well.

READ THE FOLLOWING PASSAGE AND SUGGEST HOW TO MAKE IT MORE FORMAL.

> I always like fishing. Even if I don't catch anything. It's just fun being out on the water. I like the quiet and the peacefulness. And nobody is around to bother me. I just row away from the dock, and it's like a whole other world.

HERE IS ONE WAY TO RE-WRITE THE PASSAGE.

> Fishing for pleasure is one of life's great joys, and it has been a popular pastime for centuries. Fishing allows one to relax, enjoy fresh air and sunshine, and forget about stress and pressure. Fishing develops one's sense of patience; it requires no special skills or training.

Using the third person makes the passage more formal as well as more authoritative. Short simple sentences are replaced with longer, complex sentences, which make the passage more interesting to read. Contractions and clichés are avoided. The vocabulary is more sophisticated. The final result is a text that is informed, precise and finely crafted.

IMPORTANCE OF A CONCLUDING STATEMENT IN A PERSUASIVE PASSAGE

A concluding statement is important for a persuasive passage because it sums up the main points of the passage and gives the reader a sense of completion by bringing the passage to a natural end. The concluding sentence should pull all aspects of the passage together and make sense of all the ideas, evidence, and details included previously. The concluding statement also will be somewhat inspiring since it is the writer's final attempt to convince the reader of his or her standpoint. A good concluding statement serves to cement the bonds the writer has developed with the reader.

WHAT KIND OF ARGUMENT WOULD THE FOLLOWING CONCLUDING SENTENCE BEST CONCLUDE?

> That is why it is important to have regular physical checkups with your doctor.

The sentence would make a good concluding sentence for a passage outlining reasons for seeing a doctor regularly. Such reasons might include that regular physical checkups can disclose conditions that might not be noticed, such as high blood pressure or an irregular heartbeat. Furthermore, a checkup gives the patient a chance to talk to a doctor about any problems that might exist. The doctor could order certain lab tests to check further. This concluding sentence brings all the elements of the argument together.

Informational or explanatory text

INTRODUCING A TOPIC

An informational or explanatory text should introduce the topic featured in the text. You can accomplish this by using a topic sentence followed by details supporting your thesis. Another tactic involves referring to a current event, even if your topic refers to something in history. Ideas should be organized in a logical manner, with supporting details coming right after a main concept. Connections can be made between concepts by using connecting words such as *however, since,* and *as a result.* Distinctions between ideas also should be made clear and can be signaled by words and phrases such as *but* or *on the other hand.* Furthermore, you can choose whether to include a specific relationship such as cause and effect, question and answer, or problem and solution.

Using Graphics, Formatting, and Multimedia

There are many ways to present information so it is easier to understand. Graphics are extremely useful because they present detailed information in a manner that is quickly grasped. Instead of putting the information in a paragraph, it can be fashioned into a graphic, which is much more approachable for the reader. Another useful tool is subheadings. Each subhead introduces a new concept or idea in the text and allows the reader to determine the article's main points. Multimedia, including voice over, videos, or even movies, represents another way to present information. Since movies and videos are so much a part of everyday life, most people respond very easily to this kind of presentation. Difficult material can be made much more palatable with these tools.

Developing a Topic

It is important to develop the topic in an informational or explanatory text by utilizing relevant facts that clearly support the main topic. After the introduction of the topic, supporting details should follow, including relevant facts rather than opinions. At times it may be necessary to include definitions for terms that might be unfamiliar to the reader. The cited supporting details should be concrete, which means they come from reliable sources. Quotations by experts in the field also develop the topic, and they make the text more readable and lend it variety. The results of any research also are helpful. Consider using graphics to help readers understand any technical material. Charts, multimedia techniques as well as subheads also can develop the topic.

Creating Cohesion

Appropriate transition words help clarify the relationships between ideas and concepts and create a more cohesive passage. Good writers know that such words and phrases serve to clarify the relationships between ideas and concepts. Words or phrases that show causality between ideas include *consequently, therefore,* and *as a result of. However, on the other hand, in contrast, but,* or *similarly* indicate a compare and contrast relationship. When examples of different concepts are used, words such *as namely, for example*, or *for instance* act as transition words. When it is necessary to show the order of importance of ideas or concepts, transition words such as *at first, primarily, secondly, former*, or *latter* can be used.

How could the following sentences be written with a better transition between the ideas?

They didn't know what they were doing. The boat often ran aground.

Rewriting the two sentences requires understanding the sentences' relationships with each other. In this passage, causality is suggested. The boat ran aground because they didn't know what they were doing. To combine the sentences, you need to use an appropriate transition word. This case has several options. The phrase "as a result" works well. It shows the causality between the two thoughts: "They didn't know what they were doing; as a result, the boat often ran aground." Other causality words include *because, consequently*, or *therefore.* The two sentences could be joined with any of those words, and the combination would make more sense than the separate sentences.

Using Precise Language

Writers of informational or explanatory texts must use precise language and domain-specific vocabulary in order to accurately communicate their ideas. General vocabulary words will not assert the necessary points. The reader will not follow the main idea of the passage if it lacks details supplied by carefully chosen, precise, and domain-specific language. For instance, using the term *renal* in a in a medical text is more technical than the term *kidney*. While researching a subject, you should include technical vocabulary to use during the writing of the text. Oftentimes it may be necessary to define domain-specific words for the reader.

Maintain a Formal Style

Writers of informative or explanatory passages generally use a formal style because it lends greater credence and a sense of more objectivity to the passage. The use of an informal or colloquial tone is frowned upon. Likewise, such passages generally use the third person for objectivity. Good writers use complex sentences, which are longer and add a further tone of formality and depth to the subject. By using a formal style, good writers show the seriousness of the subject; formal writing also includes clear and well-grounded supporting details. Personal opinion rarely has a place in an informative or explanatory passage, unless justified in some acceptable way.

Tell why the following excerpt is an example of a formal style.

> "Alas! the grand style is the last matter in the world for verbal definition to deal with adequately. One may say of it as is said of faith: 'One must feel it in order to know what it is.'"
>
> (Matthew Arnold, "Last Words on Translating Homer," 1873)

Matthew Arnold, a poet, commented on the "grand style," by which he means very formal writing. In so doing, he gives a good example of formal writing. Arnold uses the third person to approach his subject. He also uses precise language. His vocabulary is not simple; instead, it is on a high level. He uses the active voice rather than the passive voice. He also employs some drama, when he opens his piece with "Alas." He also tells his audience that defining the "grand style" is not an easy manner, but it can be sensed.

Having an Effective Conclusion

While a good beginning is essential, equally important to an essay, lecture, or other presentation is an effective conclusion. A good concluding statement should sum up the overall intention of the text and serve to "wrap up" the presentation so the reader is aware that you have made a logical ending to your thesis and has closure. Ideally the conclusion would review the most important points made in the presentation, the reasoning employed, and the supporting arguments for this reasoning. The conclusion builds a bridge between the presentation and the audience that helps to reassert the importance of the effort and impact the viewer's memory favorably. A good conclusion allows the reader to sit back and weigh the overall impact of the presentation.

Narratives

Establishing a Point of View

To set the stage for a narrative, introduce the reader to the setting and the characters. Next, introduce a plot line, consisting of various events that lead to a problem, climax, and resolution. This gives a narrative structure. The way the author introduces these elements is important in demonstrating the effectiveness of the narrative. Make sure to use language to describe the setting and characters so they grab the reader's interest. Make the details specific. Such a conclusion or resolution ties up the details of the story.

Introducing Characters

An author introduces characters to the reader through many means. Some authors use a description to introduce a character; other authors use an event or action to introduce a character. Still others introduce a character through the character's dialogue. In all cases, the reader receives his first impression of a character with the introduction. The reader may read a description of a character and get a sense of not only the character's appearance, but also the character's feelings. Having a character react to something also tells about a character's personality. What the character says certainly will leave an impression on the reader. Readers will be startled, amused, and saddened by characters because of their words and actions, and how the author describes them.

DETERMINE ANNA'S PROBLEM.

> Anna looked down at her hands. They were trembling. This was the third interview this week, but so far there were no job offers. Since Ted had lost his job, money was very tight. She was their only hope. When the interviewer asked her name, Anna could not speak.

Anna is nervous. We know this because her hands were trembling. She is apprehensive. The reader can tell this because this was the third job interview Anna had been on in a week, and she did not have any offers. Ted, who may be her husband, is out of work. They have very little money. She feels she is the only hope they have. The author has described Anna's problem through the words he uses and the hints he makes. Anna's problem is that she needs a job, but she can't seem to find one. Her situation is even worse because her nervousness makes her unable to speak to the interviewer.

TECHNIQUES USED BY AN AUTHOR

Authors use a variety of techniques to bring to life their narratives. Authors employ dialogue to help develop characters. The words characters speak give endless clues into their personalities as well as their conflicts and needs. Dialogue also gives the reader a sense of what is happening. Pacing is another valuable technique. Rather than have the action move along at the same pace, writers change pace according to the effect they want to achieve. To build mystery or drama, a fast pace works well; a slow pace often sets the stage before something eventful occurs. Pace is the rhythm of a narrative. Plot lines are equally important, because they provide structure in the narrative. Description can create a setting or give insight into characters. They help the reader visualize what is happening.

CREATING A COHERENT SEQUENCE OF EVENTS

A narrative's sequence of events usually emerges in order, because this is the most straightforward way to create a coherent sequence, which will not leave the reader confused. Such a structure provides a natural flow in the narrative, revealed through the dialogue and plot. A coherent sequence enhances a story, and it should never seem forced or unnatural. On the other hand, some writers change the natural order with a literary device called flashback. A flashback occurs when the writer chooses to go forward in time and then follow the natural sequence. Properly done, the flashback makes sense in the context of the story. Flashbacks can add a sense of mystery or suspense to a narrative as well as provide the reader with another literary device, foreshadowing. Nonetheless, chronological narration is used more frequently.

USING PRECISE LANGUAGE

Precise language is essential to a narrative so the story will come alive to the reader. Precise language including phrases and sensory language helps the reader imagine a place, situation, or person in the way the writer wishes. Through his or her words, the writer shapes the action of the story. Precise language should be included in the dialogue since it tells so much about the characters in a story. Sensory language can add extra detail, feeling, and color. Sensory language also appeals to the senses, so it creates a strong bond between the story and the reader.

READ THE EXCERPT.

> In the cool blue twilight of two steep streets in Camden Town, the shop at the corner, a confectioner's, glowed like the butt of a cigar.

ANALYZE THE PRECISE LANGUAGE USED IN THIS OPENING LINE FROM "THE INVISIBLE MAN" BY G. K. CHESTERTON.

This opening line is filled with precise and sensory language. The description of the "blue twilight" of two "steep" streets creates an image of a growing darkness in the streets. Here the author uses a metaphor to add color to his writing. The image of the shop that "glowed like the butt of a cigar" brings up a strong image of what the shop looked like, shining in the dark. The passage seems to suggest that only this shop was lit up. In this case, the author uses a simile comparing the shop to a lit cigar. This language draws the reader immediately into the story and leaves the reader wanting to see where the story goes from there.

ROLE OF THE CONCLUSION

As a reader's last experience with a story, a narrative's conclusion tells the most telling of all events in a story. The sense of finality in a good conclusion generally leaves the reader satisfied. Nonetheless, much of modern literature does not leave the reader satisfied, since the writer intends to leave the reader wondering what will happen next. Some writers, however, do not intend to conclude in such a way and still confuse the reader with an inadequate ending that does not relate to the events occurring in a narrative. A bad conclusion fails to resolve the conflict in the story; a good conclusion resolves the conflict even if the resolution is not one that the reader might prefer.

VLADIMIR IS WRITING A SHORT STORY ABOUT A TRIP HE MADE LAST SUMMER TO VISIT HIS GRANDMOTHER IN CHICAGO. HE HAS WRITTEN ABOUT HIS PREPARATIONS, THE TRIP, AND THE THINGS HE DID WITH HIS GRANDMOTHER. HE IS LOOKING FOR A CONCLUSION TO THE STORY. DESCRIBE WHAT VLADIMIR SHOULD LOOK FOR IN WRITING A CONCLUSION.

Vladimir should write a conclusion tying all the elements of the story together. Since he went on a trip to visit his grandmother, his short story should end with what happened when the trip ended. Such a conclusion would be the most obvious choice. Vladimir would bring the story to its close with a good ending so the reader could know what happened and what it meant to him. In this way, the reader would not be left with many questions at the end. The story's opening and its events all lead up to this point. With the addition of a good conclusion, Vladimir's story would be well crafted.

Speaking and Listening

Discussions

PREPARING FOR A GROUP DISCUSSION

A good group discussion leads to interactive learning and increases self-confidence. Careful reading of the assigned text material is important. Go over it as many times as necessary until you have a thorough understanding. Class discussions can be valuable since they promote dialogue between you and your classmates, and they also prepare you for adult life, where effective communication is essential. Think ahead of time of interpretive questions, or questions that have more than one answer. They will contribute to a lively discussion. Practice being a good listener. During the discussion, try to avoid any conflict, since conflict generally kills the discussion.

COLLEGIAL DISCUSSIONS

In well-organized collegial discussions, all students should participate actively, both listening as well as speaking. A reference such as *Robert's Rules of Order* can be quite helpful. One or two students should be appointed leader. All of the students should feel free to disagree, question, or admit when they don't understand something. Interruptions should not be allowed. It is essential that all students should come to the discussion well prepared. If disagreement occurs, the leader(s) should mediate until a consensus can be reached and facilitate the process until voting on any key issues can begin.

Questions that can be answered simply "yes" or "no" will not result in a good discussion, nor will any of the participants gain anything. Asking a question such as, "Can you give me an example?" or "What did you mean when you said...?"encourages a response which helps other students think about a subject and therefore learn. This type of communication is known as Socratic questioning, from the Greek philosopher Socrates. Questions should seek clarification, probe assumptions, probe implications, and seek clarification. The discussion moves along and the group can think about the subject, put the information together meaningfully, and create new ideas.

Class discussion guidelines should stress that everyone should be treated with respect. Whoever is leading the discussion needs to assume that everyone present has something to contribute to the discussion. No one should worry that they may say the wrong thing. Everyone should be able to understand and think critically about the assigned topic; if someone is confused, they should state the source of their confusion. Taking notes during the discussion can help you remember a point that you want to bring up later. Ideas can be challenged without resorting to personal attacks.

RESPONDING TO DIVERSE PERSPECTIVES

Every group is diverse in its own way. The opinions of others need to be respected. Perhaps in a discussion someone will bring up a perspective you had not thought of before. This perspective might help you see things differently, and you might reach a new conclusion. It is, therefore, most important that all participants listen carefully to what everyone is saying. In any discussion, the dialogue should be respectful and free of any emotional outbursts. Each participant in the group should be able to identify points of agreement and disagreement.

INTERGRATING VARIOUS SOURCES OF INFORMATION

Students must be capable of using digital media. Accordingly, he or she should be able to able to answer questions that arise with visual, quantitative, or verbal methods. Whether researching information from print sources or on the Internet, it is imperative to verify the credibility and accuracy of the information. Ask questions such as, "Can the author be connected to the subject? What are the author's qualifications, and what organizations or associations is the author connected to? Can supporting evidence be documented. Is the information current? A scholarly site, where the content is peer reviewed, is much more authoritative than an *ezine*, in which anyone can write.

Analyzing a Speaker's Point of View

The ability to analyze a speaker's point of view is an important skill, and will be important in adult life. First, examine the objective of the speech. Then, consider if the speaker comes across as knowledgeable. Examine whether the use of evidence seems logical and credible. Attempt to judge the quality of the evidence, and how clearly that evidence is presented. A good speaker uses rhetoric to persuade the audience. Faulty reasoning arises from the lack of any common sense. Ask yourself if the speaker appears dogmatic or opinionated, or if he/she is clearly and demonstrably open-minded.

Presentations

Presenting Evidence That Is Relevant and Credible

A good presentation of information should have a logical flow. It makes concrete statements rather than abstractions. Furthermore, one would present information differently to an audience of ten than to an audience of 100. Make the information useful and focused. Evidence should be relevant and supported with quotes, examples, and statistics from credible sources. Cite sources, and make sure that they are current. Important points can be repeated for effect. Using graphics at appropriate times will reinforce the argument(s) you are making. You should practice making your presentation with friends or family and listen to their critiques.

Using Digital Media to Enhance the Presentation

We live in a world of rapid change, and we need to use new tools to produce effective presentations Electronic presentations will become the norm. Web-based presentation tools can promote your audience to think visually with diagrams, charts, and maps. They also keep an audience interested and develop your reasoning and evidence. Cloud-based applications such as Prezi are replacing the standard slide show. Adding animation and music with software such as Adobe Flash greatly enhances a presentation and makes the content more memorable. As with any other presentation, it is best to practice a few times so everything flows smoothly.

Adapting Speech to a Variety of Contexts

English is a language of nuances, or subtle differences in meaning. As such, many synonyms can be utilized to attain the exact meaning you are trying to communicate, so using a thesaurus and dictionary when writing your presentation can be helpful. However, it is important that you use correct grammar and language. Maintain eye contact with the audience; if you stare off into space, your audience will lose interest quickly. Some people find it useful to begin a presentation with a joke. Whatever your style, you should project confidence and knowledge of your subject. Try your presentation out before a friend first and ask for his or her response.

Determine Why This Sentence Should Be Rewritten

They like to sail, skiing, and they also hike too.

This sentence is not in a parallel form. Instead, it is an example of faulty parallelism, since it has three different verb forms. All the verb forms in the sentence should be the same. The first verb, to sail, is an infinitive. The second is in a gerund form; the third is in present tense form. The sentence should be written so all the verbs agree: "They like to sail, to ski, and to hike, too. Now all of the verbs are in an infinitive form. Another way to write the sentence is: "They like sailing, skiing, and hiking." Now all the verbs are in a gerund form. Good writers make sure to check that their text does not contain faulty parallelism.

Language

Parallel Construction

When writing a series of words in the same form or describing the same thing, they should be in the same grammatical form. For instance, if you are using more than one verb in a sentence, the verbs must be in the same form. Also, if you are listing nouns, they must all be in the same form. The following sentence is an example of faulty parallelism, since the description of the lake is not in a parallel form. "The lake is choppy today, and it has much mud." This should be written, "The lake is choppy and muddy today," so the adjectives are parallel.

Identify and discuss the underlined phrase in the following sentence.

Their throats parched by the searing heat, the firefighters battled the blaze.

The phrase "throats parched by the searing heat" is an absolute phrase since the noun "throats" is modified by a participle phrase "parched by the searing heat" and has no relationship to the rest of the sentence, which means it does not modify anything in the main clause. The participle "being" is understood rather than stated here; the sentence could be written "Their throats being parched by the searing heat" but "being" is more commonly not stated. There are a large number of phrases other than absolute phrases; they include noun, verb, adjectival, adverbial, participial, and prepositional.

Determine the kinds of clauses found in the following sentence.

After magna hardens, it forms igneous rocks, which consist of extrusive and intrusive rocks.

This sentence contains three clauses in all. The first is "After magna hardens." This is an adverb clause because it tells when something happens. Also, it is a subordinate clause and depends on the next clause: "it forms igneous rocks." This clause is an independent clause. It can stand on its own as a sentence. The next clause "which consist of extrusive and intrusive rocks" is also a dependent clause. It cannot stand alone, because it depends on the independent clause. It is a relative clause because it tells something about the magna. Other kinds of clauses include adjective clauses and noun clauses.

Use of a Semi-Colon When Linking Two Independent Clauses

Two independent clauses can be joined by placing a semi-colon between the two clauses and frequently adding a conjunctive adverb. For instance, these independent clauses could be joined in the following manner.

One way to join these clauses is:

Jan's cell phone is new; it doesn't work very well.

However, a better way to join the clauses and clarify the relationship between them is by adding the conjunctive adverb however.

Jan's cell phone is new; however, it doesn't work very well.

There are many conjunctive adverbs, including nevertheless, still, though, also, furthermore, equally, likewise, consequently, therefore, so, and thus.

Rules for Using Colons for Lists or Quotations

Colons are used at the start of a list of items, as in the following.

My grandfather's garden has the following flowers: pansies, roses, camellias, peonies, tulips, and marigolds.

However, if the list immediately follows a verb or a preposition do not use a colon.

My grandfather's garden contains flowers *such as* pansies, roses, camellias, peonies, tulips, and marigolds.

Use a colon to introduce a long or formal quotation. A formal quotation is often preceded by such words as *these, the following*, or as *follows*.

"The Rime of the Ancient Mariner" contains this stanza:

Water, water, everywhere,

And all the boards did shrink;

Water, water, everywhere

Nor any drop to drink

Correct the spelling in the sentence below.

The chorus was barely audable over the sound of the car engine, but no one seemed aggrevated by it even though it continued throughout the performence.

The incorrectly spelled words are "audable," which should be spelled "audible;" "aggrevated," which is spelled "aggravated;" and "performance," which is spelled "performance." It is important to know how to spell words correctly. One good tool is sounding out words by breaking them into syllables. Check a word for familiar affixes. Use a dictionary to make sure you know how to spell a word. Keep word lists and use each word in a sentence. Practice with a few words at a time. Spelling rules can help as well. "I before e except after c," (receive) is one rule. Others are "drop the final e" (like, liking) and "double the last consonant" (stop, stopped) when added suffixes.

Importance of Using Style Manuals

When you write a report, story, essay, or persuasive text, you need to follow guidelines so your writing conforms to the appropriate guidelines. Two excellent sources are the *MLA (Modern Language Association) Handbook* and Turabian's *Manual for Writers.* The *MLA Handbook* is used by universities, colleges, and secondary schools as the best reference for writing a research paper. The guide gives advice on all aspects of writing research papers, from picking a topic to submitting the paper. Kate Turabian's *A Manual for Writers of Term Papers, Theses, and Dissertations* is also valuable and gives information about all aspects of writing research papers from citing sources to determining the difference between primary and secondary sources.

Rewrite the following passage so it is grammatically correct.

The title of Steinbeck's The Grapes of Wrath comes from a line in the first verse of the Battle Hymn of the Republic "He is trampling down the vintage where the grapes' of wrath are stored.

THE SENTENCE SHOULD BE WRITTEN THIS WAY:

> The title of Steinbeck's *The Grapes of Wrath* comes from a line in the first verse of the "Battle Hymn of the Republic": "He is trampling down the vintage where the grapes of wrath are stored."

The title of the Steinbeck book should be in italics; the name of the hymn should have quotation marks around it. There should be a colon before the quotation. An apostrophe is not needed after the word *grapes* since it is not in a possessive form. Finally, there should be a quotation mark at the end of the quote. These changes follow the guidelines of both the *MLA Handbook* and Turabian's *Manual for Writers.*

USING CONTEXT CLUES

In a sentence containing a new word or phrase, often the sentences before and after it can provide the reader with clues regarding the meaning of the new word or phrase. A reader can often figure out the meaning of an unknown word from these clues. For instance, a passage might say that Vanessa lived in an *affluent* neighborhood. A reader might not be familiar with the word *affluent,* but then the passage goes on to say that the neighborhood was filled with expensive homes, beautifully kept lawns, and at least three cars in the garages of each of these spacious and elegant houses. These facts give clues about the meaning of *affluent.* The reader could realize that *affluent* means rich. Another helpful clue is the placement of the word *affluent* immediately preceding a noun, *neighborhood.* This placement indicates that *affluent* likely is an adjective. As a result, the reader should look for another adjective to describe the neighborhood.

USE CONTEXT CLUES TO DETERMINE THE MEANING OF MOBILIZE IN THE FOLLOWING EXCERPT.

> Dion was determined to *mobilize* his neighbors to keep the local elementary school from closing. He trained volunteers to go to each apartment in their building and get signatures on a petition asking the board of education not to close the school. The school was saved and Dion was the neighborhood hero.

To figure out the meaning of the word *mobilize,* the reader needs to analyze the rest of the sentence as well as the following sentences. It would appear that Dion got his neighbors to take action and that the action worked. He actively trained volunteers, and they obtained signatures on the petition asking that the school not be closed. As a result, the meaning of *mobilize* becomes clearer. It means to *take action.* If you substitute *take action* for *mobilize,* the excerpt makes sense. The fact that *mobilize* is a verb also tells the reader that a synonym also needs to be a verb.

DETERMINE HOW THE CONTEXT CLUES HELP THE READER FIGURE OUT THE MEANING OF THE PHRASE TIED THE KNOT IN THE FOLLOWING EXCERPT.

> Hassan and Aisha *tied the knot* on Saturday, but they decided to postpone their honeymoon for a month. Then they will go to Florida.

While the phrase *tied the knot* might seem to have a nautical or military overtone because of the word *knot,* this is not an accurate understanding. The phrase is actually an idiom, or expression with a meaning unrelated to its literal meaning. However, the sentence containing the phrase in question contains a clue to help the reader figure out that *tied the knot* means *got married.* The clue is the word *honeymoon,* generally taken after a marriage. The reader also can figure out that the phrase's meaning is an action and that a verb would be the correct synonym for the phrase.

HOW CERTAIN ENDINGS CAN INDICATE A WORD'S PART OF SPEECH

You can tell a great deal about a word's form by examining its suffix. Certain suffixes signal that a word is a noun. One such ending is *–tion*; it forms a noun from the stem of the word complete:

completion. Other endings make a stem into an adjective. In this case the addition of *-ed* creates the adjective form of the verb, *completed.* The adverb is formed from the root word, complete with the suffix -ly. It is important to be able to analyze a word, not just for its etymology, but also for its part of speech.

Identify the part of speech of the word contender and how you made this determination.

The root word for *contender* is *contend.* The suffix *-er* indicates that the word is a noun. The suffix -*er* indicates someone who does something, so in this case it means someone who contends. If you know that the word *contend* means *compete* then you can figure out that a contender is someone who competes. If you wanted to do so, you could make the word into an adjective by adding the suffix *-ed.* The noun is formed by removing the *d* from the end of the root word and adding the suffix *-tion: contention.*

Determine the etymology of the word accentuate in the following sentence.

> Ricky liked to *accentuate* his good traits.

Without the presence of context clues in the sentence, you need to look up the word. The etymology of the word helps you discover its meaning. The dictionary says that *accentuate* is a transitive verb, that is, it has an object. This word contains four syllables: ac.cent.u.ate. The word has a Latin origin and comes from the word accentus, which means accent. When you look up the meaning of accent, you find that one of its meanings is to stress or focus attention on something. These clues provide insight into the meaning of accentuate, which means to stress or focus on something.

Using General and Specialized Reference Materials to Find the Pronunciation of a Word

A print or digital dictionary can be used as a means to discover many things about a word. It will show the correct pronunciation of a word, tell its meaning, and its part of speech. It also will tell how the word was derived, or its etymology. The dictionary has a guide that shows how to sound out the words, and lists all the parts of speech a word can be used as and the meanings it has in each form. In addition, this entry will tell you the ancient origins of the word. The thesaurus is an extremely useful tool because it lists synonyms for all the various meanings a word can have, in order to clarify the precise meaning as used in the context of a text. In this way, you can find other words to use in a report or text that mean the same as a certain overused word. Many books will have a glossary to help you with difficult or even technical words used in the text.

Read the next sentence. Figure out the meaning of conventional.

> The group of poets decided that they preferred experimenting with form rather than working in a conventional manner.

Context clues might suggest that *conventional* means usual or normal. But you may not be certain. For this reason, it is a good idea to look up words about which you are unsure in the dictionary. There you will find all the meanings of a word, and you can verify your own understanding of the word. In the dictionary there are various meanings of the word, but one seems closest to the meaning you have come up with. That meaning is "conforming to established practice or accepted standards." This meaning fits with the context of the sentence, so you have verified your understanding of the word.

Euphemism vs. Oxymoron

A euphemism is a figure of speech in which a vague, indirect, or mild word is substituted for a word deemed harsh, blunt, or offensive. For instance, people often say passed away rather than died because the former seems less offensive. Euphemisms abound in politics and society where politically correct words are used instead of words that seem pejorative. An oxymoron, on the other hand, is a figure of speech in which incongruous or contradictory terms are combined. For example, a deafening silence combines two contradictory concepts. For example, since there is no sound in silence, how can it be deafening?

DETERMINE THE FIGURE OF SPEECH USED IN THIS SENTENCE.

> "A yawn may be defined as a silent yell."(*G.K. Chesterton*, George Bernard Shaw, 1909)

The term "silent yell" is an oxymoron because a yell is not silent. These words do not belong together because these words are contradictory. By definition, an oxymoron combines two contradictory elements. Other examples include *real phony,* and *pretty ugly.* The expression is not a simile or personification, nor is it a hyperbole or onomatopoeia. Although it is a metaphor, the metaphor consists of an oxymoron.

DETERMINE HOW YOU CAN DISTINGUISH WHICH WORD IN THE SENTENCE IS A EUPHEMISM.

> Veronica went into the restaurant, was shown a table, and then asked the waiter where she could find a restroom.

This statement is very straight forward. It is about a woman entering a restaurant, sitting at the table, and asking where she could find a restroom. The word *restroom* is a euphemism for bathroom. It is considered less offensive to use the term *restroom* than the terms *bathroom* or *toilet*. This practice of softening our language has been in existence for many years. Euphemism means "the use of words of good omen" in Greek, and Greeks used euphemisms as substitutes for religious words such as the names of deities that were not supposed to be spoken. In addition, the practice was found in Indo-European languages as well as in Arabic languages. Today euphemisms are extremely popular and often are used to ensure political correctness of language.

VARIOUS NUANCES OF THE WORDS *BRAZEN* AND *DARING*

Nuances are slight differences in the meanings of words that mean almost the same thing. Nuances make a word different in its tone or shade of meaning. They are similar to connotations, although usually more subtle. In the case of the words *brazen* and *daring,* while both words mean *bold, brazen* has a slightly negative aspect having to do with being shameless, forward, or overstepping. *Daring*, on the other hand, has a more positive aspect having to do with being brave or courageous. Writers often use nuance to suggest something about a character or topic without directly stating their meaning. Readers should look for nuances in language in order to understand the writer's point of view and intent.

IMPROVING COMPREHENSION

The acquisition of general academic and domain- specific words and phrases is especially important for success in academic endeavors. Without the ability to understand language at the college or career level, a student will not be prepared for the future. Students must be familiar with domain-specific words and phrases if they hope to move on in a specific field. In order to become proficient in language, a student should make lists of new words, use them in sentences, and learn to spell them. A text book's glossary is a good source for finding domain-specific words. Extended reading allows the student to improve his or her vocabulary. Again, a good reader will try to understand the meaning of a word through context. Nonetheless, if this effort fails, the student should find the precise meaning in a dictionary or glossary.

Practice Test #1

Practice Questions

1. Which of the following might be an introduction to an essay that provides both a main idea and the importance of the idea?

a. Many colleges today require a minimum of two years of a foreign language. This is a mistake and a waste of time: more science or math courses would be better choices. After all, most students will neither live in a foreign country or need to deal with foreigners. In light of the fact that our students are behind the rest of the world in math and science, we should get rid of this archaic requirement.
b. Why do many colleges today require a minimum of two years of a foreign language? It doesn't seem like it is fair to ask students to study another language for two years. After all, this doesn't really mean that the students have two full years of study, but rather four semesters of study.
c. Many colleges today require a minimum of two years of a foreign language. This is an important requirement. Students definitely need to have at least a year of learning a foreign language. Since college admissions officers think it is important, we should, too.
d. Students don't have the option of studying a foreign language in school: they are forced to take it. They can choose from Spanish and usually one other language, like French or Chinese. Depending on the school district, some students can be involved in college-level language programs to help develop their skills.

2. In a debate, the first speaker claims that "Students should be allowed to graduate from school after completing the 10th grade, instead of making them attend until they are 18. Most students will not go to college, so it doesn't make sense to waste their time preparing for something that won't happen. These students need the extra years to start working regular jobs and supporting their families." What might be one counterclaim to this? Choose the answer that provides a counterclaim and evaluates the speaker's argument.

a. It's silly to say that students don't need to be in school until 18. A person who makes a claim like that has little understanding of the educational system and very little knowledge of real life. While it might be good to start working earlier than 18, who's to say that a student can get a good job?
b. It is certainly true that most students will never attend college. Statistics show that the majority of high school students fail to show an interest in college. There are also a high number of students who are pushed into going to college that fail the first year because they went for the wrong reasons.
c. What does a 16-year-old know about life? At 16, you live in your parents' home and are considered a child. If a student drops out at 16, there may be regrets later in life. After all, it is a proven fact that college graduates make considerably more money than workers with less education.
d. While it is true that most students do not go to college, and that working is beneficial, attending school until 18 is valuable. At 16, most students do not really know what they want to do: if they drop out of school early, they may regret that they lost the chance to study hard and attend college. Research shows that college grads make more money than those with less education.

3. Which of the following choices best completes the passage?

Standardized tests are becoming more important every year, and _______ these tests may seem like an easy way for educators to evaluate many students at once, there are considerable drawbacks. _______, teachers frequently teach to the test, which may raise scores but lowers the quality of education. ________: a recent survey showing that students know little information that is not tested on a standardized exam.

a. while, for example, case in point
b. since, while, interestingly
c. although, consequently, moreover
d. because, on the other hand, yet

4. Read the selection below, which is part of an essay given to a scholarship committee. Which of the following choices could come next? Keep in mind the style and audience.

Since before Watson and Crick first uncovered the double helix structure of DNA, companies have been trying to find ways to capitalize on the human genome. There are a number of companies that now claim to be able to trace ancestry or disease based on a small sample of blood.

a. There's simply no way to really make a lot of money this way, though. Let's face it: a company that's not profitable is not going to survive.
b. While these companies are doing their best to capitalize on people's curiosity, the high cost of the testing and analysis prevent them from expanding into the broader market.
c. These companies aren't making the grade because they are knocking on only a few doors: most folks can't afford the pricey $200 or more for some stranger to look at their blood.
d. Since these companies are targeting a small enclave, they miss out on the potential end-users who may express an interest in the noncommercial community.

5. Based on the passage in #4, what might be one possible concluding statement that provides a solution to the problem of expensive tests?

a. In summary, the high cost of curiosity is killing the DNA testing market. People simply won't shell out that much money to find out about their ancestors, and the people who are willing to are few and far between.
b. In conclusion, niche markets provide only so much growth potential for products. After that, companies need to diversify their offerings if they want to grow.
c. In summary, DNA testing kits are the wave of the future. Companies looking to capitalize on the promotion of testing kits need to find a way to make the kits affordable to the average consumer.
d. In conclusion, my business plan utilizes the current technology while partnering with local retailers to market the DNA testing kits to a broad audience while keeping the price point affordable.

6. Which of the following choices supplies an effective introduction to an essay on genetic engineering?

a. Genetic engineering refers to the modification of life via artificial methods. Genetic engineering is used in many places and in many ways. Genetic engineering is a frightening thing and this essay is about that.
b. Who hasn't heard of genetic engineering? In some ways, it is a frightful thing. This essay will examine that fear of the unknown. It will also talk about the ways that genetic engineering can be used to further enhance crop yields in Africa.
c. Fifty years ago, the average consumer would not know much about genetic engineering. However, these days, it seems as if it is on everyone's lips. This essay addresses genetic engineering. It will also examine some items created in labs by highly qualified scientists.
d. Genetic engineering: the words strike fear into many hearts. But is genetic engineering really dangerous, or is it a bogeyman created by non-scientists? This essay will describe what genetic engineering is, its applications, and deal with some of the myths about it.

7. Which of the following choices provided belongs in an essay on genetic engineering and gives an extended definition for genetic engineering?

a. It's clear what genetic engineering is: the modification of living things via modern DNA modification techniques. It's also clear what it's not: it's not the same technique farmers and animal breeders have been using for thousands of years.
b. The definition of genetic engineering is a simple one: it is the alteration of living material. While non-scientists argue about terrifying futuristic scenarios, these fears basically come from a lack of understanding.
c. What is genetic engineering? It is an unholy alliance between science, technology, and living things. Not only does genetic engineering place humanity at the top of a dangerous precipice, it does it to enhance a hidden agenda: to change who we are fundamentally.
d. Genetic engineering is a relatively modern technique developed by scientists with the hope of taking the best of the best. By getting rid of "bad" or "hurtful" material, scientists can move us toward a higher quality of life.

8. Which of the following choices best completes the passage?

Genetic engineering is not just a new way of approaching the same breeding methods used by farmers for centuries. _________, it is a completely new way of dealing with living things. _____ some scientists say that we are only working with what nature has given us, this is clearly not the case. We are not working with nature, we are creating it. We are making ourselves gods.

a. However, For example
b. On the contrary, While
c. Notably, Case in point
d. First, Second

9. Which of the following choices could be part of an essay on infectious diseases and genetic disorders? (Make sure it uses language appropriate to a science paper.)

a. What are the differences between infectious diseases and genetic disorders? You can get diseases from just about anything. You can get them from things like shaking hands. Genetic disorders are worse than infectious diseases. These are problems in a person's makeup.
b. Key differences between infectious diseases and genetic disorders are the way they are obtained. Genetic disorders are much like illogical aspects of human nature. Infectious diseases are the terrors that strike when least suspected.
c. There are key differences between infectious diseases and genetic disorders. Infectious diseases are transmitted via carriers, and include both bacterial and viral diseases. Genetic disorders are present in the DNA of the individual.
d. Infectious diseases and genetic disorders have key differences. Infectious disease can be spread from person to person via contact. One example of an infectious disease is the flu. Flu germs can remain viable for a time span that varies between hours and days.

10. Which of the following sentences best completes the selection?

The flu is a common disease that plagues millions of Americans every year. Symptoms include a runny nose, fever, coughing, and an overall feeling of achiness. While there is little that can be done once someone catches the flu, there is one important step most people fail to take to prevent themselves from getting it.

a. They don't wash their hands when they go to the bathroom.
b. They fail to do something that is vital to protecting their health.
c. They only wash their hands if someone is watching them.
d. They fail to wash their hands thoroughly and frequently

11. Which of the following choices could be a possible conclusion for the paragraph in #10?

a. In closing, if people could just try to wash their hands, they can avoid a lot of problems. They don't need to get the flu year after year.
b. In conclusion, the flu is a common infectious disease that plagues people around the world. It affects the youngest and the oldest among us most, with infant and elderly deaths highest in populations afflicted with the illness.
c. In closing, a fundamental shift needs to occur in the manner in which infectious diseases, like the flu, are addressed in the population. Public service messages on both radio and television may promote more sanitary habits.
d. In conclusion, although getting the flu is a common occurrence, it is not inevitable. Basic sanitary practices can save people pain, suffering, and a possible trip to the emergency room.

12. Which of the following choices is an example of parallel structure?

a. Ju-sung went hiking, bike riding, and sailing on his vacation; he was completely exhausted, but happy.
b. Mrs. Townsend asked us to please pick up the groceries, visit Mr. Townsend's office, and dropping the mail off at the post office.
c. Isaac and Milly spent the day at the lab performing the following tasks: cleaning the glassware, marking the new chemicals, and stock the supply closet.
d. The managers explained that they should get a loan for the business, that they should not take on a lot more debt, and to do additional financial planning to remain solvent.

13. Which of the following choices best completes the selection below?

The letter _________ explained all his hopes and dreams for my success; _______ outpouring of his love for me.

a. my grandfather, it contained an
b. from my grandfather, which containing
c. grandfather, since it contained
d. from my grandfather, it contained an

14. Which of the following choices is correct?

a. Whether the unexamined life is worth living or not; there is little doubt that people who do not carefully consider their actions often fall into difficulties.
b. There are basically two ways to live: with your conscience or moral code, which can be a difficult and painful road; or against your conscience, which may seem easy and attractive until you discover how much pain and suffering you've caused others.
c. Folding the paper over carefully so the contents were in full view; Caroline, fearful of what was coming next in the article, leaned closer to the printed page in order to more fully absorb the awful truths contained there.
d. It is unnecessary to become a philosopher to take a careful look at your existence to understand the nature of it; its application; its fundamental principles, and its future.

15. Which of the following is correct?

a. Mary had said: "I believe in the rights of my fellow man."
b. Since Fred: Jerry: and Peter wanted to go, they drove the van.
c. The Constitution: it is one of the greatest documents of all time: it is vital to our freedom.
d. Scientists need to keep finding: new sources of money to support their research:

16. Which of the following words is NOT spelled correctly?

a. Onomatopoeia
b. Fastidious
c. Meticulus
d. Minutiae

17. What is the meaning of the underlined word?

The girls sat at the table, comforting each other and sobbing through <u>lachrymose</u> stories about their own struggles with bad haircuts.

a. consolatory
b. blithe
c. mournful
d. lethargic

18. Complete the sentence below with the correct words.

After the ___________ examined the records, he gathered them up so he could discuss and _______ them with his team.

a. advocate, analysis
b. advocate, analyze
c. advocates, analyze
d. advocates, analysis

19. The following selection is from a dictionary. Which of the following sentences uses this word correctly?

NOISOME
Noi"some, a. Etym: [For noysome, fr. noy for annoy. See Annoy.]
1. Noxious to health; hurtful; mischievous; unwholesome; insalubrious; destructive; as, noisome effluvia. "Noisome pestilence." Ps. xci. 3.
2. Offensive to the smell or other senses; disgusting; fetid. "Foul breath is noisome." Shak.
-- Noi"some*ly, adv.
-- Noi"some*ness, n.

a. The noisome generated by the heavy metal rock band showed that they had not practiced in over a year.
b. Students put on masks to avoid the noisome odors issuing from the badly polluted swamp.
c. Cal's football team utilized a noisome defensive maneuver that involved having all of the running backs staying close to the quarterback.
d. Heather inhaled the noisome perfume from the bottle and smiled because the heavenly aroma was sure to please her grandmother.

Read the selection below from O. Henry's "Gift of the Magi" to answer questions 20-24:

[Della and Jim are a young husband and wife. They are very poor, and it is Christmas Eve. Della does not have enough money for a Christmas present, so she decides to sell her beautiful hair to buy a fob for Jim's watch, which once belonged to his grandfather and is his most prized possession.]

She found it at last. It surely had been made for Jim and no one else. There was no other like it in any of the stores, and she had turned all of them inside out. It was a platinum fob chain simple and chaste in design, properly proclaiming its value by substance alone and not by meretricious ornamentation—as all good things should do. It was even worthy of The Watch. As soon as she saw it she knew that it must be Jim's. It was like him. Quietness and value—the description applied to both...

When Della reached home her intoxication gave way a little to prudence and reason. She got out her curling irons and lighted the gas and went to work repairing the ravages made by generosity added to love. Which is always a tremendous task, dear friends—a mammoth task...

At 7 o'clock the coffee was made and the frying-pan was on the back of the stove hot and ready to cook the chops.

Jim was never late. Della doubled the fob chain in her hand and sat on the corner of the table near the door that he always entered. Then she heard his step on the stair away down on the first flight, and she turned white for just a moment. She had a habit of saying a little silent prayer about the simplest everyday things, and now she whispered: "Please God, make him think I am still pretty."

The door opened and Jim stepped in and closed it. He looked thin and very serious. Poor fellow, he was only twenty-two—and to be burdened with a family! He needed a new overcoat and he was without gloves.

Jim stopped inside the door, as immovable as a setter at the scent of quail. His eyes were fixed upon Della, and there was an expression in them that she could not read, and it terrified her. It was not anger, nor surprise, nor disapproval, nor horror, nor any of the sentiments that she had been prepared for. He simply stared at her fixedly with that peculiar expression on his face.

Della wriggled off the table and went for him.

"Jim, darling," she cried, "don't look at me that way. I had my hair cut off and sold because I couldn't have lived through Christmas without giving you a present. It'll grow out again—you won't mind, will you? I just had to do it. My hair grows awfully fast. Say 'Merry Christmas!' Jim, and let's be happy. You don't know what a nice—what a beautiful, nice gift I've got for you."

"You've cut off your hair?" asked Jim, laboriously, as if he had not arrived at that patent fact yet even after the hardest mental labor.

"Cut it off and sold it," said Della. "Don't you like me just as well, anyhow? I'm me without my hair, ain't I?"

Jim looked about the room curiously.

"You say your hair is gone?" he said, with an air almost of idiocy.

"You needn't look for it," said Della. "It's sold, I tell you—sold and gone, too. It's Christmas Eve, boy. Be good to me, for it went for you. Maybe the hairs of my head were numbered," she went on with sudden serious sweetness, "but nobody could ever count my love for you. Shall I put the chops on, Jim?"

Out of his trance Jim seemed quickly to wake. He enfolded his Della. For ten seconds let us regard with discreet scrutiny some inconsequential object in the other direction...Jim drew a package from his overcoat pocket and threw it upon the table.

"Don't make any mistake, Dell," he said, "about me. I don't think there's anything in the way of a haircut or a shave or a shampoo that could make me like my girl any less. But if you'll unwrap that package you may see why you had me going a while at first."

White fingers and nimble tore at the string and paper...

For there lay The Combs—the set of combs, side and back, that Della had worshipped long in a Broadway window. ...They were expensive combs, she knew, and her heart had simply craved and yearned over them without the least hope of possession. And now, they were hers, but the tresses that should have adorned the coveted adornments were gone.

But she hugged them to her bosom, and at length she was able to look up with dim eyes and a smile and say: "My hair grows so fast, Jim!"

...Jim had not yet seen his beautiful present. She held it out to him eagerly upon her open palm. The dull precious metal seemed to flash with a reflection of her bright and ardent spirit.

"Isn't it a dandy, Jim? I hunted all over town to find it. You'll have to look at the time a hundred times a day now. Give me your watch. I want to see how it looks on it."

Instead of obeying, Jim tumbled down on the couch and put his hands under the back of his head and smiled.

"Dell," said he, "let's put our Christmas presents away and keep 'em a while. They're too nice to use just at present. I sold the watch to get the money to buy your combs. And now suppose you put the chops on."

20. What is the theme in this selection?

a. True love leads to the sacrifice of one's own most precious possessions.
b. Christmas is the representation of the love and sacrifice needed by all.
c. The love between two people eventually leads to difficult circumstances.
d. Sacrifice without love is meaningless, but may lead to deeper feelings later.

21. Which detail below best supports the idea that Jim loves Della?

a. Jim asks, ""You've cut off your hair?"
b. Jim had gone to work that day and came home on time.
c. Jim sat down on the couch and smiled.
d. Jim says, "I sold the watch to get the money to buy your combs."

22. Della is concerned about what her husband will do when he sees her hair is gone. What is one important idea that Della learns after her husband comes home?

a. He considers her sacrifice worthless
b. He is shocked that she would sell her hair.
c. He loves her regardless of her appearance.
d. He has sold his watch to buy combs for her.

23. What might be one reason O. Henry included the exact dialogue between Della and Jim?

a. He was trying to show how Della and Jim might have decided to choose a different solution to the money issue.
b. He wanted to illustrate that they were not well-educated and that they were just average people.
c. He wanted to show that Della was from a certain area of the city and that Jim was obviously from another town.
d. He was trying to set up the story for what would come when Della revealed that she had cut off her hair.

24. Which of the following choices best illustrates the way O. Henry builds tension in the story?

a. It was even worthy of The Watch. As soon as she saw it she knew that it must be Jim's.
b. The door opened and Jim stepped in and closed it. He looked thin and very serious.
c. Jim looked about the room curiously. "You say your hair is gone?" he said, with an air almost of idiocy.
d. Jim was never late. Della doubled the fob chain in her hand and sat on the corner of the table near the door that he always entered.

25. What is one effect the setting of the novel had on the story in Victor Hugo's *Les Miserables*?

a. It was set during the time period just before the tempestuous French Revolution, and it created a new world and new rules for the characters to follow.
b. It was set after the period of the stormy French Revolution, and it added to the feeling of helplessness and lawlessness in the novel.
c. It was set some time after the terrible French Revolution, and it developed the ongoing theme of helplessness in the face of overwhelming odds.
d. It was set almost one hundred years before the terrors of the French Revolution, and it helped to explain how the oppression of the underclass led to eventual revolt.

26. Below is the poem "The Donkey" by G. K. Chesterton. Compare it to the painting of Balaam and the Donkey by Rembrandt. What is one key idea expressed in both works?

The Donkey - G. K. Chesterton

When fishes flew and forests walked
And figs grew upon thorn,
Some moment when the moon was blood
Then surely I was born.
With monstrous head and sickening cry
And ears like errant wings,
The devil's walking parody
On all four-footed things.
The tattered outlaw of the earth,
Of ancient crooked will;
Starve, scourge, deride me: I am dumb,
I keep my secret still.
Fools! For I also had my hour;
One far fierce hour and sweet:
There was a shout about my ears,
And palms before my feet.

a. The donkey is the devil's creation, and its stubbornness is carefully depicted in both works.
b. The donkey is usually seen as a slow animal, and both works depict the donkey as moving swiftly toward a goal.
c. The donkey is seen as a disgusting pack animal, and both works indicate that the donkey is indeed a lowly animal.
d. The donkey is typically seen as lowly, but both works depict the donkey as being a more elevated creature because of its actions.

27. In the modern play, *West Side Story*, two members of rival gangs meet and fall in love. The outcome of their relationship leads to tragedy. What classical work does this most resemble?

a. *Macbeth*
b. *The Taming of the Shrew*
c. *Romeo and Juliet*
d. *A Midsummer Night's Dream*

Read the selection from George Washington's Farewell Address to answer questions 28-32:

The Unity of Government, which constitutes you one people, is also now 9
dear to you.—It is justly so; for it is a main Pillar in the Edifice of your real independence; the support of your tranquility at home; your peace abroad; of your safety; of your prosperity in every shape; of that very Liberty, which you so highly prize.—But as it is easy to foresee, that, from different causes, and from different quarters, much pains will be taken, many artifices employed, to weaken in your minds the conviction of this truth;—as this is the point in your political fortress against which the batteries of internal and external enemies will be most constantly and actively (though often covertly and insidiously) directed it is of infinite moment, that you should properly estimate the immense value of your national Union to you collective and individual happiness;—that you should cherish a cordial, habitual, and immovable attachment to it; accustoming yourselves to think and speak of it as of the Palladium of your political safety and prosperity; watching for its preservation with jealous anxiety; discountenancing whatever may suggest even a suspicion, that it can in any event be abandoned, and indignantly frowning upon the first dawning of every attempt to alienate any portion of our Country from the rest, or to enfeeble the sacred ties which now link together the various parts.

For this you have every inducement of sympathy and interest.—Citizens by 10
birth or choice of a common country, that country has a right to concentrate your affections.—The name of AMERICAN, which belongs to you, in your national capacity, must always exalt the just pride of Patriotism, more than any appellation derived from local discriminations. With slight shades of difference, you have the same Religion, Manners, Habits, and Political Principles. You have in a common cause fought and triumphed together; the Independence and Liberty you possess are the work of joint counsels, and joint efforts—of common dangers, sufferings, and successes.—

But these considerations, however powerfully they address themselves to your sensibility, are greatly outweighed by those which apply more immediately to your Interest. Here every portion of our country finds the most commanding motives for carefully guarding and preserving the Union of the whole.

28. Which of the following choices best supports the idea that Washington was concerned about the preservation of the Union?

a. "But these considerations, however powerfully they address themselves to your sensibility, are greatly outweighed by those which apply more immediately to your Interest."
b. "With slight shades of difference, you have the same Religion, Manners, Habits, and Political Principles."
c. "Here every portion of our country finds the most commanding motives for carefully guarding and preserving the Union of the whole."
d. "For this you have every inducement of sympathy and interest.—Citizens by birth or choice of a common country, that country has a right to concentrate your affections."

29. Which of the following is a key idea supported and developed in the Farewell Address?

a. The preservation of the current peace depends entirely on local actions.
b. The unity of the government is entirely at the will of the people that it governs.
c. Citizens should protect the harmony of the United States, and actively support it.
d. People who participate in discrimination of any kind are enemies of the state.

30. How does Washington connect the rights and privileges of citizens to the preservation of the Union?

a. By noting that the preservation of the Union may be under attack and that the average citizen needs to turn his attention to governing.
b. By first mentioning the value of being a citizen and then indicating that patriotism should not support discrimination .
c. By showing that this country is one that allows its citizens privileges not found in many others and that government is by the will of the people.
d. By mentioning that citizens need to keep a sharp eye on the government and develop an interest in the history of its policies.

31. What does the phrase "concentrate your affections" mean?

a. your desire for love
b. your feeling of joy
c. your deepest loyalty
d. your longing for the Union

32. What are some of the goals in this section of Washington's Farewell Speech?

a. to show that the privilege of citizenship has come at a high price and is to be valued
b. to show that citizens should be proud and need to fight foreign interests
c. to highlight the idea that the government can take over and dissolve the Union
d. to encourage citizens to value their liberties and to preserve the Union

Read the selection from Franklin Delano Roosevelt's 1941 State of the Union Address to answer questions 33- 36:

Many subjects connected with our social economy call for immediate improvement. As examples:

We should bring more citizens under the coverage of old-age pensions and unemployment insurance. We should widen the opportunities for adequate medical care. We should plan a better system by which persons deserving or needing gainful employment may obtain it.

I have called for personal sacrifice. And I am assured of the willingness of almost all Americans to respond to that call. A part of the sacrifice means the payment of more money in taxes. In my Budget Message I will recommend that a greater portion of this great defense program be paid for from taxation than we are paying for today. No person should try, or be allowed, to get rich out of the program; and the principle of tax payments in accordance with ability to pay should be constantly before our eyes to guide our legislation. If the Congress maintains these principles, the voters, putting patriotism ahead of pocketbooks, will give you their applause.

In the future days, which we seek to make secure, we look forward to a world founded upon four essential human freedoms. The first is freedom of speech and expression—

everywhere in the world. The second is freedom of every person to worship God in his own way—everywhere in the world. The third is freedom from want—which, translated into world terms, means economic understandings which will secure to every nation a healthy peacetime life for its inhabitants—everywhere in the world. The fourth is freedom from fear—which, translated into world terms, means a world-wide reduction of armaments to such a point and in such a thorough fashion that no nation will be in a position to commit an act of physical aggression against any neighbor—anywhere in the world.

That is no vision of a distant millennium. It is a definite basis for a kind of world attainable in our own time and generation. That kind of world is the very antithesis of the so-called new order of tyranny which the dictators seek to create with the crash of a bomb. To that new order we oppose the greater conception—the moral order. A good society is able to face schemes of world domination and foreign revolutions alike without fear.

Since the beginning of our American history, we have been engaged in change—in a perpetual peaceful revolution—a revolution which goes on steadily, quietly adjusting itself to changing conditions—without the concentration camp or the quick-lime in the ditch. The world order which we seek is the cooperation of free countries, working together in a friendly, civilized society.

This nation has placed its destiny in the hands and heads and hearts of its millions of free men and women; and its faith in freedom under the guidance of God. Freedom means the supremacy of human rights everywhere. Our support goes to those who struggle to gain those rights and keep them. Our strength is our unity of purpose. To that high concept there can be no end save victory.

33. Which statement best supports the idea that FDR believed that America is constantly evolving toward a better situation?

a. Since the beginning of our American history, we have been engaged in change—in a perpetual peaceful revolution—a revolution which goes on steadily, quietly adjusting itself to changing conditions—without the concentration camp or the quick-lime in the ditch.
b. This nation has placed its destiny in the hands and heads and hearts of its millions of free men and women; and its faith in freedom under the guidance of God.
c. To that new order we oppose the greater conception—the moral order. A good society is able to face schemes of world domination and foreign revolutions alike without fear.
d. The fourth is freedom from fear—which, translated into world terms, means a world-wide reduction of armaments to such a point and in such a thorough fashion that no nation will be in a position to commit an act of physical aggression against any neighbor—anywhere in the world.

34. Read the following selection from a blog entry on FDR's speech. What aspect of the speech is emphasized?

> ...There is, of course, a lot to love in the speech. It highlights the important social issues of the day, the very same issues our nation is struggling with at the moment. What can we do about our elderly? Do class distinctions matter? The fact of the matter is, no one wants to take care of a sickly aging relative, regardless of class. Then again, most of our elderly don't want to live with their offspring, either—rich or poor. It begs the question...

a. It emphasizes the need for a social safety net for the aging populace.
b. It emphasizes the need for a lack of social class distinctions.
c. It highlights the fact that many of the elderly do not want long-term care.
d. It highlights the idea that people want to live independently.

35. In this text, FDR claims that raising taxes will result in a patriotic populace that will happily support the government. What might be one argument against this idea?

a. Americans are uninterested in pursuing freedom of any kind, and the four freedoms listed here are not considered important.
b. The average citizen already feels overburdened by taxes and feels the money is not being well-spent by the government.
c. Individuals will easily assent to the idea of a greater tax burden since it will naturally lead to a more prosperous state.
d. Patriots of all kinds are part of the natural makeup of America, and some will feel that the support of government is something that should be contemplated and debated.

36. What is a major theme that Roosevelt articulates in his speech?

a. It is important for all people to have access to the benefits of an old-age system that supports citizens when they can no longer work.
b. Patriotic people will feel the need to pay more taxes to the government in order to obtain certain benefits they would not be able to afford.
c. People who want to work should be able to find work without bias and without undue hardship.
d. There are four basic freedoms that are vital to the health of people: speech, worship, freedom from want, and freedom from fear.

37. Your history club is engaging in a discussion on George Washington. You were assigned Washington's Farewell Address and need to elucidate an aspect of Washington's character from that selection. Which of the following might be a good contribution to the discussion?

a. Washington's character can be seen in his construction of his aptly titled Farewell Address. The address was written to inform his audience about his convictions.
b. Washington had a high regard for the unity of America and put his faith in the power of the regular citizens to preserve it.
c. George Washington was a man among men. His deep-held belief that there should be no discrimination of any kind was a key aspect of his character.
d. It can be clearly seen that Washington's character was vacillating: he was convinced of the necessity of government but unwilling to indicate his preference for its type.

38. Your history club needs to come up with a topic for the following semester. Which is the best choice for developing a topic that allows all members of the group to have a say?

a. Members can vote via secret ballot, and the majority will decide.
b. Members can shout out what they want at meetings.
c. Members should accept whatever topic is decided on by the leadership.
d. Members should consult a teacher to find out what to study.

39. In a discussion on the American recession (which, according to technical indicators, ended some time ago), which of the following questions would serve to propel the debate forward and clarify the issues?

a. Since the recession ended a long time ago, why don't we all feel a lot better about the situations we are in?
b. The technical indicators show that the recession ended some time ago; what are those technical indicators?
c. We can clearly see that the recession did not end a long time ago, and that the idea of a recession is the creation of politicians. Why do we keep voting for the same people who got us into this mess?
d. If the recession ended some time ago, why are the unemployment numbers still up and why are businesses not hiring at the rates they did in other recessions?

40. In a discussion on local laws, one of your classmates indicated that, "No one should be allowed to drink extra large sodas. They are really bad for you and make you fat! We should ban all large sodas." Which of the following choices would be a thoughtful counter-response that could be a part of the broader discussion?

a. Sodas are full of empty calories and we should ban them. As a matter of fact, we should ban everything with sugar or corn syrup. I think that candy, soda, chips, and other junk food should not be allowed in our nation. We are becoming a nation of overeaters.
b. While it is true that sodas are full of empty calories, many people do enjoy them in moderation. Making a law to control what people eat or drink goes against the idea of personal liberty, and takes away the freedom of the individual.
c. That's a ridiculous idea. That's the problem with most people like you: you don't think through the real issues and get to the heart of the problem. You just want to legislate everything all the time, and living in a nanny state might sound great to you, but the fact of the matter is, you won't like it when they start regulating what you like to eat or do.
d. The conclusion drawn by my classmate addresses a serious issue that reaches to the heart of public safety: the regulation of health concerns. A major health concern is what is consumed. Is the population consuming nutritious foods to bolster our nation's health?

41. You are preparing for a class discussion on a local issue: should the town acquire a wetland in order to protect it? You have access to two sources of information:

1) A retired physics professor, being interviewed on a morning news show, mentions: "It's obvious that our town needs to buy this land. We have to protect what we have from greedy developers who only want to turn a profit."

2) An article written by an ecologist on a well-known news site notes: "It is in our best interest to purchase this land. Wetlands are disappearing and there are not enough private donors to help with their protection."

Evaluate the views in both sources. Which source provides the best material for your assignment?

a. It may be true that some businesses profit from buying up wetlands; however, the important point is that wetlands are disappearing. An ecologist noted that there are not enough private donors to buy these places.
b. Greedy businesses are at the heart of the problem: they simply want to buy up cheap land to build and make money. They don't care about destroying our natural treasures. The physics professor noted that our town needs to buy this land.
c. It's clear that wetlands are endangered; they are going to disappear unless we do something about it. We should get private donors to buy the land. An ecologist noted that wetlands are in danger.
d. Businesses are part of the wetland problem. Without developers to buy them up, the town would not need to purchase the land to protect it. A physics professor noted that the wetland problem is related to greed.

42. A speaker says, "HealthNut Nutritional Supplements are good for your blood pressure. Doctors indicate that high blood pressure is a real problem in America." What type of fallacy does this illustrate?

a. red herring
b. hasty generalization
c. faulty appeal to authority
d. appeal to people

43. You are given the following information and need to develop a speech. Which of the following choices organizes the information in an effective, logical way?

*1933: Hitler becomes the chancellor of Germany
*1939: Nazi troops invade Poland using Blitzkreig, or "lightning war"
*1919: The Treaty of Versailles was signed, which may have helped lead Germany toward war
*1935: Hitler begins military conscription

a. The road to World War II was long and bitter. It certainly began when the Treaty of Versailles was signed in 1919. Hitler rose to power easily and began implementing his own ideas for a master race. In 1939, the Nazi soldiers attacked Poland.
b. What started World War II? The blame can certainly fall on the rise of Hitler and the Nazi party. Hitler rose to power in 1933. He and his political party railed against the Treaty of Versailles that was signed in 1919. This caused problems for Germany. In 1939, the Nazis invaded Poland.
c. Germany began the road to World War II when the Treaty of Versailles was signed in 1919; the conditions in it were very harsh. Hitler rose to power in 1933 and began conscripting troops in 1935, showing that the country was getting ready for war. In 1939, the Nazis invaded Poland.
d. The military push into Poland was just the beginning of the conquest. In World War II, Hitler had a tight grip over his country. He first came to power in 1933. His rise may have been due to the Treaty of Versailles that was signed in 1919.

44. A story needs to introduce a clear point of view and a problem. Which of the following choices would be a good start to a story?

a. Madeline gazed out the window and sighed. The sun was blazing forth in all its glory and the wind was blowing in the trees. She could see horses frolicking in the fields just beyond the border of the schoolhouse.
b. Peter adjusted his helmet and gripped the reins tightly. He prepared himself for the jump that was to come: Jupiter, his trusty horse, didn't fail him. The duo made it over the obstacle easily.
c. The broken vase lay on the floor, with hundreds of glittering pieces scattered about. The water had darkened the rug. The flowers had not yet begun to gasp, but they looked ugly and crushed.
d. Henry and Youngsook looked at the sheet of paper in the desk. The columns were full of numbers and letters. Suddenly, Youngsook turned to her friend; her face was white. "This is Mrs. Thompson's missing answer sheet. Henry, it's in *your* desk!"

45. Which of the following best develops the story?

a. Youngsook slammed the desk closed. "Henry! That's the missing answer sheet!" Henry turned beet red. "I know, I know. Now what?"

b. Youngsook's mind raced back to the summer camp where she met Henry. She had caught him stealing food from the kitchen, and the incident eventually led to them becoming great friends. It was more than ten years ago, and Henry had never done anything like that again. Or did he?

c. The answer sheet rested inside Henry's desk like a body in a shallow grave. The answer sheet created all sorts of problems. It raised all kinds of questions, too. Youngsook looked at her friend's face. It had gone from beet red to a pale gray.

d. "Youngsook, do you remember that time I visited you in Seoul?" Henry asked. Youngsook nodded. "Yeah, that was great. We had a lot of fun skating in the indoor rink." Henry smiled. "Those were good times. Do you remember Ho-won? He called me the other day! He wants to stay with me again. He told me that he has something important that he needs to tell you."

46. Read the story below. Which of the following choices builds toward the logical conclusion?

Reggie lifted the lid and gazed into the pot. It was as he had suspected: his mother was cooking up a batch of her famous chicken stew. Reggie glanced out the kitchen window and then leaned back to see if his mother was in the laundry room. All clear! Slowly, Reggie gripped the large cup and dropped it into the bubbling brew. He drew out the steaming fluid and turned toward the counter to grab his spoon.

a. Reggie started to eat the soup. It was really good. Then Reggie's mom surprised him by coming up the basement stairs.

b. "Reggie! Come help me open this basement door!" Reggie heard his mother shout. He hid the cup under a large towel.

c. "Reginald Bernard Wilson! You put that soup down right now young man!" And Reggie did—the cup dropped from his startled grip and shattered on the floor.

d. Reggie lifted the cup to his lips and then paused. He heard a sound. It was like a soft plodding noise, and it was getting ever closer.

47. Which of the following choices paints the most vivid picture of the scene?

a. Carly paused; she caught her breath and reached for her camera. Hanging in the air nearby was a tiny hummingbird.

b. Carly froze mid-step; she sucked in the cool morning haze and grasped her camera. A hummingbird was nearby.

c. Carly paused; she sucked in the air and grabbed at her camera. She saw a small hummingbird.

d. Carly froze mid-step; she breathed in the cool morning haze and lifted her Komodo HiShot. There, flitting from flower to flower, was a tiny ruby-breasted hummingbird.

48. Use the story that began in #44. Which of the following choices could provide a summary of the plot and a satisfactory conclusion?

a. Mrs. Thompson's answer sheet is gone! Everyone thinks that Mrs. Thompson simply misplaced it; she does have a reputation for being absentminded. However, the answer sheet was put in Henry's desk by Maritza. She wanted to frame Henry so she could win a scholarship. Youngsook and Henry follow the clues to find out who put the answer sheet in his desk. Eventually, Mrs. Thompson finds out about the whole incident.

b. The scholarship contest is heating up—who will win? Henry and his nemesis Maritza are neck and neck. When Mrs. Thompson's answer sheet disappears, all of the students think it was simply lost—until it shows up in Henry's desk. However, the answer sheet was put in Henry's desk by Maritza. She wanted to frame Henry so she could win a scholarship. Maritza finally tells Mrs. Thompson about the answer sheet and the story ends.

c. When Mrs. Thompson's answer sheet disappears, all of the students think it was simply lost—until it shows up in Henry's desk. It's clear that someone knows about Henry's theft at camp over ten years ago. After following the clues, Henry and his best friend Youngsook uncover the truth: Maritza planted the answer sheet in Henry's desk. She had been in competition with Henry for a scholarship and was hoping to get him disqualified. Youngsook and Henry confront Maritza, who confesses and then tells the teacher. Henry goes on to win the scholarship.

d. Maritza framed Henry. Then she told the teacher about it. Youngsook and Henry searched for clues. They found out that Maritza knew about Henry's past. They all told Mrs. Thompson together. The end of the story comes when Maritza finally confesses to her insidious crime. Youngsook and Henry are best friends, so they trust each other. Youngsook knows that Henry did not take the answer sheet, so she helps find the real criminal.

49. Which of the following choices best supplies part of an essay on ancient history?

a. Middle Eastern history is dominated by great empires. This aids our understanding of the region and provides insight into the cultures. People frequently discuss the Romans and Greeks. The great empires of the Assyrians and Babylonians also shaped this area.

b. The rule of the Assyrians was one of power and might. The Assyrians and Babylonians, their successors, strongly believed in relocation: they would move captured populations from one region to another. Would the Romans have put up with such a practice?

c. The succession of these empires completely dominates our understanding of ancient Middle Eastern history. History texts frequently gloss over them quickly, but that brevity belies the enormity of each empire's impact. The Assyrians, Babylonians, Persians, Greeks, and Romans were all dominating forces with uniquely intertwined cultures.

d. The empires of the Middle East are key to its development. Little can be said of Middle Eastern history to a certain point without including the vast machinations of power players such as the Assyrians and Greeks. Although the Neo-Babylonian Empire did not last as long as its predecessor, it can be seen to have had far-reaching impacts on other cultures.

50. Your instructor has asked you to rewrite the following sentences to make them clearer. Which choice shows the most effective corrections?

I want to study engineering when I go to college, because engineering is really cool, and my mom is an engineer. I don't want to just do any kind of thing tho I want to study mechanical. That's the best for me.

a. I want to study engineering when I go to college. I think engineering is interesting; and my mom is an engineer. I want to study mechanical engineering, because I think it's the best kind of engineering.
b. I want to study engineering when I go to college. I think engineering is interesting, and my mom is an engineer. I want to study mechanical engineering because I think it's the best kind of engineering.
c. I want to study engineering; when I go to college because engineering is interesting. My mom is an engineer. I want to study mechanical engineering.
d. I want to study engineering when I go to college; because engineering is really cool, and my mom is an engineer. I don't want to just do any kind of thing though I want to study mechanical engineering. That's the thing best for me.

51. What might be one way to make effective use of technology to develop a team writing project?

a. Use your phone to text ideas about the paper to your team members. Ask your teacher to use the computer lab to research the assignment.
b. Use a blog to communicate your ideas; develop a website dedicated to the construction of your assignment.
c. Use email to communicate with other team members and develop a page on your school's website to track the progress of the assignment. Each student should have access to this page.
d. Use a word-processing program to write your paper. Print out copies and share them with your team members so they can add or change the work.

52. You need to elucidate an outline for a 25-page research report. Which of the following choices would best broaden the topic listed below?

Topic: How Science Affects Us

a. How Science Affects Us: 1) introduction 2) science helps us understand 3) science helps us stay healthy 4) science helps us fight disease 5) science is all around us 6) science is good 7) conclusion
b. How Science Affects Us: 1) science helps us understand the world around us (general overview) 2) science is important (relevant to life) 3) science is good (good stuff) 4) science is helpful (helpful stuff) 5) science helps us stay healthy (no soda or chips) 6) science helps us understand stuff 7) conclusion
c. How Science Affects Us: 1) overview 2) science helps us understand the world around us 3) science helps us invent new things (airplanes, harvesting machines) 4) science helps us improve on things (better cars, planes) 5) science helps us stay healthy (improved nutrition, exercise) 6) science helps us fight disease (medicines, practices) 7) conclusion
d. How Science Affects Us: 1) overview 2) science helps us avoid conflict 3) science helps develop weapons 4) science helps us improve crop yields 5) science helps us stay healthy 6) science helps us fight disease 7) conclusion

53. Your teacher has assigned you a research project on ancient Persian culture. Which of the following sources would be a good starting point that provides the most accurate information?

a. the Wikipedia "Persian Culture" entry
b. "All Cool Persian Stuff": a blog written by a scientist
c. *An Overview of Persian Society*: a book written by a historian
d. "Uncovering the Secrets of Persia": a two-page magazine article about lost temples

54. Dante Alighieri's *Divine Comedy* is divided into three parts: the inferno, the purgatorio, and the paradiso. Which of the following choices reflects the original source material for at least one of the divisions?

a. the Tao Te Ching's humility and wisdom
b. the Koran's Five Pillars of Islam
c. the Bible's hell and heaven
d. the discourses of Buddha

55. Use the context to determine the meaning of the underlined word. Which choice is most similar in meaning to the underlined word?

Tears streaming down, Josefina ran to the teacher. She was received with open arms and a sympathetic ear. The perpetrator of the tears was quickly collared, protesting his innocence. Still, to be fair, Mrs. Smirnoff allowed him to make his case. However, when Ivan began to relate his confused version of events, Mrs. Smirnoff sighed and rolled her eyes; Ivan's <u>glib</u> testimony was exactly what she had come to expect from the biggest troublemaker in school.

a. quick and easy, usually in a disingenuous manner
b. sincere and honest, usually in a straightforward way
c. confusing and incoherent, usually in a despondent manner
d. repenting and sorrowful, usually in an affecting way

56. Read the sentence below. What is the meaning of the underlined word?

One of the historians referred to the US actions taken against the hostile movements of the North Korean government as a "police action." That <u>police action</u> was to eventually cost the US 30,000 American lives.

a. armed conflict or war
b. military occupation
c. civilian defense operations
d. treaty development

Answers and Explanations

ELA-Literacy.W.9-10.1a

1. A: Many colleges today require a minimum of two years of a foreign language. This is a mistake and a waste of time: more science or math courses would be better choices. After all, most students will neither live in a foreign country or need to deal with foreigners. In light of the fact that our students are behind the rest of the world in math and science, we should get rid of this archaic requirement.

This argument introduces the main argument, that colleges should drop the language requirement, and includes support for the author's idea: students should spend more time in math and science courses because US students lag behind all other nations. The other choices either introduce claims that are not supported or details that lack a specific main idea.

ELA-Literacy.W.9-10.1b

2. D: While it is true that most students do not go to college, and that working is beneficial, attending school until 18 is valuable. At 16, most students do not really know what they want to do: if they drop out of school early, they may regret that they lost the chance to study hard and attend college. Research shows that college grads make more money than those with less education.

This choice provides a counterclaim while acknowledging the truth in the speaker's argument. Choice A opens with an ad hominem attack and fails to assert a counterclaim. Choice B lacks a counterclaim. Choice C lacks an acknowledgment of what the speaker claimed.

ELA-Literacy.W.9-10.1c

3. A: This is the best choice for this passage because an idea is introduced, and then there is a change in the direction. The change in direction acknowledges another point of view. The next sentence illustrates part of the author's argument with a supporting idea (standardized tests lower the quality of education). The last sentence is talking about a specific example and using the colon to break up the sentence.

ELA-Literacy.W.9-10.1d

4. B: While these companies are doing their best to capitalize on people's curiosity, the high cost of the testing and analysis prevent them from expanding into the broader market.

This is the best choice. It maintains a formal presentation style while utilizing common business terms. The other choices either fail to establish a formal style (Choices A and C), or do not use the correct terminology (Choice D).

ELA-Literacy.W.9-10.1e

5. D: In conclusion, my business plan utilizes the current technology while partnering with local retailers to market the DNA testing kits to a broad audience while keeping the price point affordable.

This conclusion best supports the initial ideas or suggestions laid out in #4. These ideas (DNA testing kits are expensive and appeal to a niche market) are addressed here and explain what the student wanted to state: that he has a business plan to provide inexpensive tests to a broader audience. Choice A is too informal and does not address a solution. Choice B is too vague and does not cover the information in #4. Choice C acknowledges the issues but offers no concluding solution.

ELA-Literacy.W.9-10.2a

6. D: Genetic engineering: the words strike fear into many hearts. But is genetic engineering really dangerous, or is it a bogeyman created by non-scientists? This essay will describe what genetic engineering is, its applications, and deal with some of the myths about it.

An effective essay needs to open with the statement of a clear topic and it needs to organize the essay in a coherent manner. This is the only choice that grabs the reader's attention and then mentions the organization of the paper. Choice A gives a definition for genetic engineering but fails to establish a cohesive structure for the essay. Choice B uses specifics in the introduction, and Choice C is not well-organized.

ELA-Literacy.W.9-10.2b

7. A: It's clear what genetic engineering is: the modification of living things via modern DNA modification techniques. It's also clear what it's not: it's not the same technique farmers and animal breeders have been using for thousands of years.

This is the best choice because it provides a concise but extended definition of genetic engineering. Choices B and C do not provide an extended definition of genetic engineering and only develop an argument. Choice D contains part of an extended definition but is missing details (like the modification of DNA).

ELA-Literacy.W.9-10.2c

8. B: The transitions needed here must complete the sentences while preserving the direction of the passage. The first sentence gives us one direction, then the second sentence provides a contradiction. The third sentence is about what scientists are saying, but includes a contrasting comment.

ELA-Literacy.W.9-10.2d

9. C: There are key differences between infectious diseases and genetic disorders. Infectious diseases are transmitted via carriers, and include both bacterial and viral diseases. Genetic disorders are present in the DNA of the individual.

This choice uses science-based language appropriate to a biology paper. Choices A and B do not use domain-appropriate language. Choice D discusses diseases but not genetic disorders.

ELA-Literacy.W.9-10.2e

10. D: This is the only choice that matches the style and tone of the passage. Choices A and C are too informal. Choice B does not complete the passage.

ELA-Literacy.W.9-10.2f

11. D: In conclusion, although getting the flu is a common occurrence, it is not inevitable. Basic sanitary practices can save people pain, suffering, and a possible trip to the emergency room.

This choice best matches the style in the paragraph from #10. It also provides an adequate conclusion for the topic by noting that the flu is not inevitable. Choice A is too informal and doesn't match the style of the paragraph. Choice B only discusses details about influenza. Choice C deviates from the ideas discussed in the passage and introduces new information.

ELA-Literacy.L.9-10.1a

12. A: Ju-sung went hiking, bike riding, and sailing on his vacation; he was completely exhausted, but happy.

Parallel structure refers to using consistent word patterns in the same sentence. The sentence needs to be consistent throughout. The first sentence tells us everything Ju-sung did (hiking, bike riding, sailing), which form a consistent pattern. The other choices all fail to develop this pattern in the usage of verbs and in the usage of clauses.

ELA-Literacy.L.9-10.1b

13. D: from my grandfather, it contained an

This sentence contains a prepositional phrase and an independent clause separated off the main sentence via semicolon. This is the only choice that uses correct grammar. A prepositional phrase starts with a preposition and usually ends with a gerund, noun, pronoun, or clause.

ELA-Literacy.L.9-10.2a

14. B: There are basically two ways to live: with your conscience or moral code, which can be a difficult and painful road**;** or against your conscience, which may seem easy and attractive until you discover how much pain and suffering you've caused others.

A semicolon links two (or more) independent clauses. It can also be used to avoid confusion when listing items. Choice B is listing items and using the semicolon to avoid a misunderstanding. Choices A and C combine a dependent and independent clause. Choice D incorrectly mixes commas and semicolons in the list.

ELA-Literacy.L.9-10.2b

15. A: This is the only choice that uses the colon correctly; it introduces a quotation. The other choices do not use the colon in the correct way to introduce either a quotation or a list of items.

ELA-Literacy.L.9-10.2c

16. C: This word should be spelled "meticulous."

ELA-Literacy.L.9-10.4a

17. C: mournful

The meaning of *lachrymose* is *mournful* or *tearful*. The context of the sentence shows that the girls are upset (they are crying and comforting each other) in connection with the unpleasant subject (bad haircuts) of the stories.

ELA-Literacy.L.9-10.4b

18. B: advocate, analyze

The pronoun used in the sentence indicates that the subject will be one man, so this disqualifies "advocates." The second part of the sentence indicates that the man is going to take some kind of action, so the blank needs to be completed with a verb ("analyze," in this case, since analysis is the noun form).

ELA-Literacy.L.9-10.4c

19. B: Students put on masks to avoid the noisome odors issuing from the badly polluted swamp.

Noisome refers to something that is unwholesome or putrid. Only Choice B uses it in this fashion; Choice A relates it to noise and uses it as a noun. Choice C incorrectly uses the adjective, and Choice D treats the word as its antonym.

ELA-Literacy.RL.9-10.2

20. A: True love leads to the sacrifice of one's own most precious possessions.

The entire story is about how Della and Jim are deeply in love. They both sell something important to themselves to buy a present for the other person.

ELA-Literacy.RL.9-10.1

21. D: He says, "I sold the watch to get the money to buy your combs."

Jim's most prized possession was his grandfather's watch. He sold it to purchase the combs for his wife. Choice A deals with Jim's shock—his wife no longer has her beautiful hair for which he just bought expensive combs. Choice B is something that Jim did consistently, and Choice C does not provide support to the idea.

ELA-Literacy.RL.9-10.3

22. C: He loves her regardless of her appearance.

Jim obviously loves Della, proving that she had nothing to worry about. "Out of his trance Jim seemed quickly to wake. He enfolded his Della...

"Don't make any mistake, Dell," he said, "about me. I don't think there's anything in the way of a haircut or a shave or a shampoo that could make me like my girl any less." Jim hugs her tightly and then says that nothing could change his feelings for her. Choice A is the opposite of what Jim feels, Choice B deals with the shock Jim feels, but does not answer the question about what Della learns from her husband, and Choice D is about what Jim did before he got home. It does not show what Della learned.

ELA-Literacy.RL.9-10.4

23. B: He wanted to illustrate that they were not well-educated and that they were just average people.

This story is about the love and sacrifice of two average individuals. The dialogue is given to show that Della and Jim were not highly educated or particularly special: they were just in love.

ELA-Literacy.RL.9-10.5

24. C: Jim looked about the room curiously. "You say your hair is gone?" he said, with an air almost of idiocy.

In the beginning of the story, Della has her hair cut off so she can get money for Jim's gift. However, she is worried about how she will appear to her husband and is concerned that he will be very angry (or worse). When Jim keeps asking about Della's hair, it almost seems as if he *is* angry about it.

ELA-Literacy.RL.9-10.6

25. B: It was set after the period of the stormy French Revolution, and it added to the feeling of helplessness and lawlessness in the novel.

A major theme in Hugo's book is how one can change; it is related to the chaos that appears as the backdrop of the novel. The period of time after the French Revolution was tempestuous. It helped heighten the character development and eventual change of Jean Valjean. The other choices are incorrect because they do not indicate the correct time period or the correct theme development.

ELA-Literacy.RL.9-10.7

26. D: The donkey is typically seen as lowly, but both works depict the donkey as being a more elevated creature because of its actions.

In Rembrandt's painting, the donkey is laying down with its head raised. It is depicting the story of Balaam. Balaam was riding on his donkey when the animal suddenly refused to go forward. After beating the animal, the donkey spoke and Balaam's eyes were opened: an angel with a sword was waiting to kill Balaam. The donkey had saved Balaam's life. The poem mentions the donkey's elevated status when it carried Jesus into Jerusalem before his execution on the cross. Both works depict the donkey in a more positive light than it is typically given in popular culture. The donkey is typically seen as stupid and stubborn.

ELA-Literacy.RL.9-10.9

27. C: Romeo and Juliet

Romeo and Juliet is the story of two star-crossed lovers, and the *West Side Story* was modeled on it. *The Taming of the Shrew* is about the relationship between a man and his wife, *Macbeth* is about a man seizing power, and *A Midsummer Night's Dream* is a comedic love story.

ELA-Literacy.RI.9-10.1

28. C: "Here every portion of our country finds the most commanding motives for carefully guarding and preserving the Union of the whole."

This sentence clearly indicates that the Union may be under some sort of threat: Washington uses the word *guarding*, showing that there was the possibility of attack. The other choices contribute to Washington's theme, but they do not clearly illustrate the uneasiness found in this sentence.

ELA-Literacy.RI.9-10.2

29. C: Citizens should protect the harmony of the United States, and actively support it.

This part of the speech addresses Washington's concern over the unity of the nation He indicates that the privileges enjoyed by citizens should not be taken for granted. Choices A and B do not address the main theme of this selection. Choice D is a distortion of one of Washington's ideas.

ELA-Literacy.RI.9-10.3

30. B: By first mentioning the value of being a citizen and then indicating that patriotism should not support discrimination.

Washington unpacks his points by first noting the privilege of being a citizen and then mentioning that discrimination can be a possible obstacle to preserving the Union. The other choices mention ideas that are found in the passage, but they are not part of the connection between the rights of citizens and the preservation of the budding nation.

ELA-Literacy.RI.9-10.4

31. C: your deepest loyalty

Washington wrote in a style not typically utilized today. From the context of the surrounding sentences, it is clear that he is hoping that regular people turn their hearts toward their country and have the highest regard for it. The other choices focus more on the individual's feelings for himself.

ELA-Literacy.RI.9-10.5

32. D: to encourage citizens to value their liberties and to preserve the Union

This is the focus of this selection. Choice A only mentions one goal. Choices B and C are taken from some of the details in the passage.

ELA-Literacy.RI.9-10.6

33. A: Since the beginning of our American history, we have been engaged in change—in a perpetual peaceful revolution—a revolution which goes on steadily, quietly adjusting itself to changing conditions—without the concentration camp or the quick-lime in the ditch.

This is the only statement listed here that directly supports the idea that FDR thought that America is constantly moving toward a better way of life.

ELA-Literacy.RI.9-10.7

34. A: It emphasizes the need for a social safety net for the aging populace.

While the other ideas in Choices B and C are clearly mentioned in the blog, they are not derived from the speech. Choice A is the only one that discusses an idea that shows up in the speech.

ELA-Literacy.RI.9-10.8

35. B: The average citizen already feels overburdened by taxes and feels the money is not being well-spent by the government.

The argument that needs to be evaluated is that people will be happy to give more money in taxes to the government. It would be safe to raise the counterargument that the general population may already believe they are paying enough in taxes and don't think the government is spending that money wisely. Not everyone will be happy to give more to the government to spend. Choices A and D do not address the question. Choice C actually agrees with FDR's premise.

ELA-Literacy.RI.9-10.9

36. D: There are four basic freedoms that are vital to the health of people: speech, worship, freedom from want, and freedom from fear.

This speech is typically referred to as the "Four Freedoms" speech. In it, FDR articulates the basic freedoms he believes in. These freedoms are the central focus of the speech, since it supports the other ideas that he is focusing on (i.e., social issues). Choice A is a detail in the speech, Choice B is not articulated, and Choice C is not in the speech.

ELA-Literacy.S.9-10.1a

37. B: Washington had a high regard for the unity of America and put his faith in the power of the regular citizens to preserve it.

This is the only choice that is supported by the text above. Choice A tells us nothing about Washington's character. Choice C distorts a part of the speech that addresses the issues between people from different areas of the country. Choice D is a misunderstanding of Washington's ideas.

ELA-Literacy.S.9-10.1b

38. A: Members can vote via secret ballot, and the majority will decide.

While consulting a teacher is a great idea, it does not allow for all of the members to have a say in the decision-making process (Choice D). Choice B will result in arguments and wasted time. Choice C does not allow for other members to have their voices heard.

ELA-Literacy.S.9-10.1c

39. D: If the recession ended some time ago, why are the unemployment numbers still up and why are businesses not hiring at the rates they did in other recessions?

This is the best choice because it clarifies some important ideas related to the topic and encourages open debate over the understanding of statistics. Choice A is too vague. Choice B asks about technical indicators, which may or may not be a familiar topic; it also does not encourage varying points of view in a discussion. Choice C is off-topic and encourages a political debate, rather than a discussion on the recession.

ELA-Literacy.S.9-10.1d

40. B: While it is true that sodas are full of empty calories, many people do enjoy them in moderation. Making a law to control what people eat or drink goes against the idea of personal liberty, and takes away the freedom of the individual.

This is the best choice because it acknowledges the other person's ideas while effectively elaborating on one's own ideas in a respectful manner that draws on the knowledge of American founding documents. Choice A does little to advance the discussion, instead just chiming in with the original speaker with one's own ideas. Choice C is an ad hominem attack, which has no place in a civil discussion; it also does not address the topic. Choice D acknowledges the argument but makes no counter-response.

ELA-Literacy.S.9-10.2

41. A: It may be true that some businesses profit from buying up wetlands; however, the important point is that wetlands are disappearing. An ecologist noted that there are not enough private donors to buy these places.

This choice addresses the issue, uses information from both sources, but puts the emphasis on the qualified viewpoint (which is that of the ecologist; a physics professor may be smart, but ecology is not his field of expertise). Choice B puts the emphasis on the unqualified professional, Choice C misinterprets the information provided by the expert, and Choice D does not address the issue, but addresses a side issue related to the problem.

ELA-Literacy.S.9-10.3

42. A: red herring

The fallacy illustrated here is a "red herring" because it does not indicate what this has to do with the nutritional supplements. Instead, it distracts the listener with the fact that high blood pressure is a real problem—which may be true, but does not support the initial claim made by the speaker.

ELA-Literacy.S.9-10.4

43. C: Germany began the road to World War II when the Treaty of Versailles was signed in 1919; the conditions in it were very harsh. Hitler rose to power in 1933 and began conscripting troops in 1935, showing that the country was getting ready for war. In 1939, the Nazis invaded Poland.

This is the best choice since it put historical events in chronological order. The other choices take events out of order or skip important information entirely.

ELA-Literacy.W.9-10.3a

44. D: Henry and Youngsook looked at the sheet of paper in the desk. The columns were full of numbers and letters. Suddenly, Youngsook turned to her friend; her face was white. "This is Mrs. Thompson's missing answer sheet. Henry, it's in *your* desk!"

This is the only choice that introduces characters and a plot. Choices A and B are about character development, but have no problem. Choice C has a problem, but no character is introduced.

ELA-Literacy.W.9-10.3b

45. B: Youngsook's mind raced back to the summer camp where she met Henry. She had caught him stealing food from the kitchen, and the incident eventually led to them becoming great friends. It was more than ten years ago, and Henry had never done anything like that again. Or did he?

This choice uses reflection to move the story along. Henry just found the answer sheet in his desk. There was an incident in his past where he had stolen something. This connects with the story to show that Henry may (or may not) have taken the answer sheet. Choice A is a dialogue that does not move the story forward with any new information. Choice C provides a description, but does not supply anything new. Choice D introduces multiple plot lines but does not help move the story forward.

ELA-Literacy.W.9-10.3c

46. C: "Reginald Bernard Wilson! You put that soup down right now young man!" And Reggie did—the cup dropped from his startled grip and shattered on the floor.

A variety of techniques are used here to move the story forward. The narrative in the selection helps to set the stage. The brief monologue helps develop the tension and build toward the conclusion of the story. This is the only choice that develops the story and provides a satisfactory conclusion. Choice A is too short and abrupt; it doesn't match the style of the selection. Choice B doesn't develop tension or come to a conclusion. Choice D creates tension but does not build to a conclusion.

ELA-Literacy.W.9-10.3d

47. D: Carly froze mid-step; she breathed in the cool morning haze and lifted her Komodo HiShot. There, flitting from flower to flower, was a tiny ruby-breasted hummingbird.

This choice provides the most description. It allows the reader to know the time of day (early morning), the temperature (cool, not cold), the kind of camera Carly had (a fancy one), and the action and the color of the hummingbird. The other choices contain elements of these descriptions but are not complete.

ELA-Literacy.W.9-10.3e

48. C: When Mrs. Thompson's answer sheet disappears, all of the students think it was simply lost—until it shows up in Henry's desk. It's clear that someone knows about Henry's theft at camp over ten years ago. After following the clues, Henry and his best friend Youngsook uncover the truth: Maritza planted the answer sheet in Henry's desk. She had been in competition with Henry for a scholarship and was hoping to get him disqualified. Youngsook and Henry confront Maritza, who confesses and then tells the teacher; Henry goes on to win the scholarship.

This choice provides a comprehensive summary that includes important points and gives a strong conclusion that reflects the issues going on in the story. It shows how Youngsook and Henry's friendship survives and how they find the true culprit in the crime, and it wraps up the story with the truth coming out and Henry winning the scholarship. The other choices do not include important information or fail to provide an adequate sequence that leads to the summary of the conclusion.

ELA-Literacy.W.9-10.4

49. C: The succession of these empires completely dominates our understanding of ancient Middle Eastern history. History texts frequently gloss over them quickly, but that brevity belies the enormity of each empire's impact. The Assyrians, Babylonians, Persians, Greeks, and Romans were all dominating forces with uniquely intertwined cultures.

This choice provides a coherent writing style that follows the chronology of the empires. Choice A does not follow chronological order and leaves out important information. Choice B gives detailed information about a certain idea, but fails to provide a sufficient overview of the topic. Choice D lacks focus and coherence.

ELA-Literacy.W.9-10.5

50. B: I want to study engineering when I go to college. I think engineering is interesting, and my mom is an engineer. I want to study mechanical engineering because I think it's the best kind of engineering.

This choice fixes the run-on sentence, correctly uses punctuation, and modifies the language so it is more formal (and fit for a classroom assignment). The other choices all contain grammar errors.

ELA-Literacy.W.9-10.6

51. C: Use email to communicate with other team members and develop a page on your school's website to track the progress of the assignment.

This choice effectively uses technology to communicate (via email) and to show the progress of the assignment (via webpage). Email allows for quick communication, while the webpage can be updated so changes to the assignment can be seen in real-time. The other choices are not effective uses of technology in developing a project.

ELA-Literacy.W.9-10.7

52. C: How Science Affects Us: 1) overview 2) science helps us understand the world around us 3) science helps us invent new things (airplanes, harvesting machines) 4) science helps us improve on things (better cars, planes) 5) science helps us stay healthy (improved nutrition, exercise) 6) science helps us fight disease (medicines, practices) 7) conclusion

This is the best choice because it provides an outline for the information; it narrows the topic into subsections and provides detailed information for those sections. The other choices are either too vague or do not provide an adequate essay structure.

ELA-Literacy.W.9-10.8

53. C: *An Overview of Persian Society*: a book written by a historian

While the other sources may have reliable information, a book on the research topic is usually a good way to start. Books typically get researched by the author and then vetted by a team of editors. A printed book is more likely to contain accurate information than a webpage. A blog can contain accurate information, but the blog listed in Choice B is not written by an expert in the field. Choice D is too narrow for the topic at hand.

ELA-Literacy.W.9-10.9a

54. C: The Bible's Hell and Heaven

The *Divine Comedy* is a story of a man who visits three places: hell, purgatory, and heaven. He is led by Virgil. The Bible mentions both heaven and hell, and this is where Dante drew his source material for his story.

ELA-Literacy.L.9-10.4d

55. A: quick and easy, usually in a disingenuous manner

From the context of the paragraph, we can see that there has been an incident (Josefina is crying). We can also see that she is well-received by the teacher; the person responsible for the tears is located and allowed to tell his side of the story, but we soon learn that the teacher knows he is a troublemaker. He most likely caused a problem and is now trying to cover it up; his story does not ring true (it is "confused" and, of course, "glib.")

ELA-Literacy.L.9-10.5a

56. A: armed conflict or war

This is an example of a euphemism, or words that mean something other than their literal meaning. This selection makes a reference to the Korean War, which may be understood from the context (over 30,000 American lives lost). Choice B is about troops coming and staying in a place, which cannot be derived from the passage. Choice C is a literal reading of the euphemism. Choice D is about a peaceful operation.

Practice Test #2

Practice Questions

1. Which of the following choices is an example of parallel structure?

a. I bought the new speech recognition software for my computer.
b. When the book finally came out, it was first sold to local stores, and then was selling on the open market.
c. The new phone can perform a large number of tasks quickly, precisely, and efficiently.
d. Mrs. Hampton asked her students to take their time—to complete the test slowly, in detail, and thoughtfully.

2. Which of the following choices best completes the sentence?
_____________, there's no way you can be a part of the swimming relay competition.

a. Unless you find a new partner
b. You have a new partner
c. When it is time
d. As you can find a partner

3. Which of the following choices shows the best way to punctuate the sentence?

a. I packed a picnic to take to the park with my friends; I made sure that I brought all of the plates and cups, too.
b. I packed a picnic to take to the park with my friends, I made sure that I brought all of the plates and cups, too.
c. I packed a picnic to take to the park with my friends I made sure that I brought all of the plates and cups, too.
d. I packed a picnic to take to the park with my friends: I made sure that I brought all of the plates and cups, too.

4. Which of the following choices best completes the sentence?
It's easy to have disagreements over political issues, but I remain committed

a. to the important ideal laid out by Patrick Henry; "Give me liberty, or give me death."
b. to the important ideal laid out by Patrick Henry? "Give me liberty, or give me death."
c. to the important ideal laid out by Patrick Henry "Give me liberty, or give me death."
d. to the important ideal laid out by Patrick Henry: "Give me liberty, or give me death."

5. Which of the following words is spelled incorrectly?

a. salubrious
b. sureptitious
c. artifice
d. requisition

6. Which of the following choices shows a citation written in the MLA style?

a. Smith, John. Reason and Thought in the Modern Age; Chicago; Juggernaut, 2010. Print
b. Smith, John. Reason and Thought in the Modern Age. Chicago: Juggernaut, 2010. Print.
c. Smith, John. Reason and Thought in the Modern Age. Chicago; Juggernaut, 2010. Print.
d. Smith, John. Reason and Thought in the Modern Age. Chicago. Juggernaut; 2010. Print.

7. Using the context of the selection below, what is the meaning of the underlined word?

The discussion over the new park had begun well, but it soon descended into an <u>acrimonious</u> debate over misuse of tax revenues.

a. shocking
b. childish
c. rancorous
d. revealing

8. Which of the following choices best completes the sentence?

Natalie reviewed the notes carefully, with one eye on the judge's _________ and another eye on the _______ of the decision. There was certainly more than one way to ________ the case.

a. interpretation, evolve, interpret
b. interpretation, evolution, interpret
c. interpret, evolution, interpretation
d. interpretation, evolution, interpretation

9. What is the etymology of the word below?

ELEGIT

> E*le"git, n. Etym: [L., he has chosen, fr. eligere to choose. See Elect.] (Law) Defn: A judicial writ of execution, by which a defendant's goods are appraised and delivered to the plaintiff, and, if not sufficient to satisfy the debt, all of his lands are delivered, to be held till the debt is paid by the rents and profits, or until the defendant's interest has expired.

a. It was derived from legal and judicial terms.
b. It was derived from Latin and French.
c. It was derived from eligere and elect.
d. It was derived from a judicial writ.

10. Use the dictionary entry from #9 to help you determine the meaning of the word in the sentence. Which of the following choices is most similar in meaning to the underlined word?

> <u>Writs of elegit</u> seemed highly unfair to those who were in debt (although, it probably didn't seem that way to the creditor, who was basically cordoning off the debtor's property so he might collect), and were completely abolished in 1956.

a. a legal argument
b. a special tax
c. a debt collector's receipt
d. a judicial statement

11. What are the underlined words an example of?

Although there have been overwrought denials and saber-rattling, the North Koreans' nuclear program is an <u>open secret</u>.

a. oxymoron
b. paradox
c. onomatopoeia
d. euphemism

12. Which of the following choices best matches the feeling of the sentence?

Jeb climbed the rickety steps to the broken front screen and knocked. His eyes wandered over the bleak landscape and dead fields. A tired cow munched what was left of the parched field. A ________ chicken halfheartedly clucked near the ruined barn.

a. willowy
b. scrawny
c. thin
d. slim

13. Which of the following words/phrases are key in understanding the meaning of the following selection from G. K. Chesterton's *Eugenics and Other Evils*?

> I publish these essays at the present time for a particular reason connected with the present situation; a reason which I should like briefly to emphasize and make clear.
>
> Though most of the conclusions, especially towards the end, are conceived with reference to recent events, the actual bulk of preliminary notes about the science of Eugenics were written before the war. It was a time when this theme was the topic of the hour; when eugenic babies (not visibly very distinguishable from other babies) sprawled all over the illustrated papers; when the evolutionary fancy of Nietzsche was the new cry among the intellectuals; and when Mr. Bernard Shaw and others were considering the idea that to breed a man like a cart-horse was the true way to attain that higher civilization, of intellectual magnanimity and sympathetic insight, which may be found in cart-horses. It may therefore appear that I took the opinion too controversially, and it seems to me that I sometimes took it too seriously. But the criticism of Eugenics soon expanded of itself into a more general criticism of a modern craze for scientific officialism and strict social organization.
>
> And then the hour came when I felt, not without relief, that I might well fling all my notes into the fire. The fire was a very big one, and was burning up bigger things than such pedantic quackeries. And, anyhow, the issue itself was being settled in a very different style. Scientific officialism and organization in the State which had specialized in them had gone to war with the older culture of Christendom. Either Prussianism would win and the protest would be hopeless, or Prussianism would lose and the protest would be needless. As the war advanced from poison gas to piracy against neutrals, it grew more and more plain that the scientifically organized State was not increasing in popularity. Whatever happened, no Englishmen would ever again go nosing round the stinks of that low laboratory. So I thought all I had written irrelevant, and put it out of my mind.
>
> I am greatly grieved to say that it is not irrelevant.

a. briefly to emphasize and make clear, actual bulk of preliminary notes, organization in the State, all I had written irrelevant
b. I felt, not without relief, that I might well fling all my notes into the fire, Prussianism, Christendom, I sometimes took it too seriously
c. greatly grieved, Eugenics, the war advanced from poison gas to piracy against neutrals, most of the conclusions
d. I publish these essays at the present time for a particular reason, Eugenics, greatly grieved, not irrelevant

Read the following selection from Macbeth to answer questions 14–21:

A cry within of women.

What is that noise?

Seyton. It is the cry of women, my good lord.

Macbeth. I have almost forgot the taste of fears;

The time has been, my senses would have cool'd
To hear a night-shriek; and my fell of hair
Would at a dismal treatise rouse and stir
As life were in't: I have supp'd full with horrors;
Direness, familiar to my slaughterous thoughts
Cannot once start me

Re-enter Seyton.

Wherefore was that cry?

Seyton. The queen, my lord, is dead.

Macbeth. She should have died hereafter;

There would have been a time for such a word.
To-morrow, and to-morrow, and to-morrow,
Creeps in this petty pace from day to day
To the last syllable of recorded time,
And all our yesterdays have lighted fools
The way to dusty death. Out, out, brief candle!
Life's but a walking shadow, a poor player
That struts and frets his hour upon the stage
And then is heard no more: it is a tale
Told by an idiot, full of sound and fury,
Signifying nothing.

Enter a messenger.

Thou comest to use thy tongue; thy story quickly.

Messenger. Gracious my lord,

I should report that which I say I saw,

But know not how to do it.

Macbeth. Well, say, sir.

Messenger. As I did stand my watch upon the hill,

I look'd toward Birnam, and anon, methought,

The wood began to move.

Macbeth. Liar and slave!

Messenger. Let me endure your wrath, if't be not so:

Within this three mile may you see it coming;

I say, a moving grove.

Macbeth. If thou speak'st false,

Upon the next tree shalt thou hang alive,

Till famine cling thee: if thy speech be sooth,

I care not if thou dost for me as much.

I pull in resolution, and begin

To doubt the equivocation of the fiend

That lies like truth: 'Fear not, till Birnam wood

Do come to Dunsinane:' and now a wood

Comes toward Dunsinane. Arm, arm, and out!

If this which he avouches does appear,

There is nor flying hence nor tarrying here.

I gin to be aweary of the sun,

And wish the estate o' the world were now undone.

Ring the alarum-bell! Blow, wind! come, wrack!

At least we'll die with harness on our back.

14. In what way does the text show that Macbeth feels his doom is approaching?

a. Ring the alarum-bell! Blow, wind! come, wrack!
b. If thou speak'st false, Upon the next tree shalt thou hang alive,
c. At least we'll die with harness on our back.
d. She should have died hereafter;

15. What is one of the themes in Shakespeare's *Macbeth*?

a. the corruption of humanity through bribery
b. the destruction of the soul through the unbridled pursuit of power
c. the discovery of the innermost parts of the human soul
d. the comedy of errors that result from miscommunication

16. How does Macbeth change from the beginning of the play until the end?

a. He begins as a noble, loyal hero of land and becomes a murderer who understands the outcome of his actions.
b. He begins as a bloodthirsty murderer who only wants power and ends as a tragic hero aware of his impending doom.
c. He begins as the quintessential anti-hero and progresses toward his own redemption as the play unfolds.
d. He begins as a loyalist to the current king and then begins to doubt his position in the kingdom.

17. What does Macbeth mean when he says, "Life's but a walking shadow"?

a. Life is a reflection of man's waking moments.
b. Life is walking like a shadow.
c. Life is dark and fleeting.
d. Life is full of darkness.

18. Which of the following scenes from *Macbeth* serves to build tension and develop a turning point?

a. the scene where Lady Macbeth washes her hands
b. the scene where King Duncan enquires about his commanders
c. the scene where Macbeth hears his wife has died
d. the scene where Macbeth sees Banquo's ghost

19. Compare the government in Shakespeare's *Macbeth* to that in the United States. Although there are significant cultural differences between the two, what is one key similarity between them?

a. Both systems involve nonelected heads of state to serve as the main power broker between other lesser governing bodies.
b. Rulers in both systems require the support of the immediate members of the government or ruling class in order to govern effectively.
c. A key similarity between the two systems is that both have duly elected officials put in place by the common people.
d. The main power of both systems lies in the conscription of soldiers into the military and a system of rewards for those men.

20. In Act I, Scene 3, lines 39–47 of *Macbeth*, Banquo meets the three witches and speaks the following lines:

Banquo:

So wither'd and so wild in their attire,

That look not like the inhabitants o' the earth,

And yet are on't? Live you? or are you aught

That man may question? You seem to understand me,

By each at once her choppy finger laying

Upon her skinny lips: you should be women,

And yet your beards forbid me to interpret

That you are so..

Compare this description of the sisters to the painting *The Three Witches* by Fuseli. This painting, completed after 1783, shows three middle-aged women in long hoods and cloaks. They appear to be almost hairless. What can be said about the depictions of the sisters in these two works?

a. The depiction of the sisters in the painting is different from that in the play, since the women have beards in the play and are almost hairless in the painting.
b. They both depict the sisters as working over a boiling hot pot and working their evil magic.
c. The depiction of this scene in the painting is of Banquo considering the women while the women look evilly at him.
d. The painting shows the three sisters as actually being closer to monsters, while the play indicates that they are clearly women.

21. In Act 1, Scene 7, Macbeth has just assented to the murder of the king. He says:

"If it were done when 'tis done, then 'twere well
It were done quickly: if the assassination
Could trammel up the consequence, and catch
With his surcease success; that but this blow
Might be the be-all and the end-all here,
But here, upon this bank and shoal of time,
We'ld jump the life to come. But in these cases
We still have judgment here; that we but teach
Bloody instructions, which, being taught, return
To plague the inventor: this even-handed justice
Commends the ingredients of our poison'd chalice
To our own lips. He's here in double trust;
First, as I am his kinsman and his subject,
Strong both against the deed; then, as his host,
Who should against his murderer shut the door,
Not bear the knife myself. Besides, this Duncan
Hath borne his faculties so meek, hath been
So clear in his great office, that his virtues
Will plead like angels, trumpet-tongued, against

The deep damnation of his taking-off;
And pity, like a naked new-born babe,
Striding the blast, or heaven's cherubim, horsed
Upon the sightless couriers of the air,
Shall blow the horrid deed in every eye,
That tears shall drown the wind. I have no spur
To prick the sides of my intent, but only
Vaulting ambition, which o'erleaps itself
And falls on the other."

Which person may Macbeth be comparing himself to?

a. Virgil, the spiritual guide to Dante in The Divine Comedy
b. Judas Iscariot, the man who betrayed Jesus in the New Testament
c. Ulysses, the mythical king who constructed the Trojan horse in Greek mythology
d. Penelope, the wife of the king in Ovid's Heroides (Heroines)

22. Which of the following choices introduces a specific claim and distinguishes it from counterclaims?

a. Is texting while driving really a critical safety issue? Are all kinds of distracted driving created equal? What can be said about the nature of distracted driving among teenagers?
b. It's true that distracted driving is dangerous. There may be nothing more dangerous than texting while driving. Texting while driving has resulted in more than 15,000 deaths and over 200,000 injuries. The majority of texting drivers are teens, although other age groups have been implicated.
c. Texting while driving is one of the key issues facing young people today: it's a fact that texting drivers have killed over 16,000 people between 2002 and 2007. While some people claim that any kind of distracted driving is dangerous, texting beats them all by keeping attention away from the road.
d. Driving and texting have gone hand in hand ever since the first teen decided that he needed to let his friends know what he was thinking right then and there. Government offices have kept tabs on distracted drivers, and the numbers are staggering. The years of the study were from 2002 to 2007.

23. Which of the following might be a counterclaim to the idea that all distracted driving (i.e., putting on makeup, eating, talking on the phone, texting, etc.) is the same?

a. Driving and texting don't mix. It is a dangerous combination on par with other forms of distracted driving, such as eating or talking to friends on the phone.
b. Should texting while driving even be legal? While some authorities may want to stop the practice in its entirety, it may be difficult to enforce.
c. Distracted driving in any form is lethal. Texting while driving is worse than other kinds of distracted driving. It should be made illegal and carry heavy fines.
d. Texting while driving is more dangerous than driving while eating or talking on the phone because the driver's eyes are no longer on the road.

24. Which of the following choices best completes the sentences?

Texting while driving is something that many teenagers do, which may be a reason why officials want to ________ as destructive juvenile behavior. ______ is texting while driving more dangerous than eating while driving? The evidence certainly supports this conclusion, ______ an insurance company's poll of distracted drivers.

a. crack down on it. it's seen / Since / according to
b. crack down on it—it's seen / But / according to
c. crack down on it; it's seen / Although / accordingly
d. crack down on it: it's seen / So / according

25. Which of the following sentences would NOT fit into a passage on distracted driving that is being presented as a formal report?

a. However, while government statistics may seem cold and unfeeling, the testimonies of broken families are not.
b. No one likes distracted drivers. They are not that smart. They could kill someone. They don't think about others.
c. Distracted driving claims hundreds of lives every day, leaving a trail of broken dreams in its wake.
d. Authorities are considering new statues to govern the use of cell phones in vehicles and are now providing police with equipment that can remotely shut off phones.

26. Which of the following provides a satisfactory conclusion to an opinion piece on distracted driving?

a. While it's clear that distracted driving in any form is dangerous, texting while driving is particularly lethal. It is now up to citizens to organize an effective method for managing this practice while balancing individual rights.
b. Distracted driving is the bane of teenagers. Since it is difficult to convince many of them that the practice is bad, there may be something more needed.
c. Texting while driving is more dangerous than other kinds of driving. After all, what are you doing when you are texting? You are not paying attention to the road.
d. Since distracted driving is probably going to be around for a long time, it's not going to go away. Teens, middle-aged people, and senior citizens are all going to be engaged in some kind of distracted activity.

27. Which of the following choices might be the best way to begin a research paper for your science class about nutrition and digestion?

a. Include an introductory paragraph about the process of digestion and how it relates to nutrition. Include a heading showing that it is the introduction and a graphic illustrating a person eating.
b. Explain the complexities of digestion, including how specific enzymes break down particular molecules, like those of protein or carbohydrates. Show a chart with the enzymes and their molecules.
c. Use a series of graphics that show how digestion works. Use a brief statement under each caption to identify what part of the process is being described.
d. Write a brief introduction about how food is affected by the various processes in the human body. Explain in detail how each process works and include an account of what happens when food is ready to exit the body.

28. Which of the following quotes might fit into a research paper on nutrition and digestion and provides supporting information to the reader?

a. "I don't know what it is, but it tastes good," Professor King smiles. "But what is the effect it has on my body?
b. "Digestion is a serious process. It encompasses a whole world that we don't really understand," says noted yoga master Hans Smith.
c. "The simple fact of the matter is, you are what you eat," noted nutritionist Danny Kaye.
d. "We must choose whole foods for a whole life. People need to abandon their cravings for potato chips and dig into some good soybeans," said Mrs. Castle, the librarian.

29. Which of the following choices best complete the passage?

> The digestive process is well understood and can be easily explained. __________, most people are not interested in it since they have the uncomfortable feeling that the speaker may soon turn to that hot topic of what they put in their mouths. ____________ that digestion is the key to our body functions, we should not shirk our understanding of it. __________people get a good understanding of digestion, they will begin to naturally make beneficial food choices.

a. Finally / Since / Admittedly
b. First / Second / Third
c. Furthermore / In regards to / Since
d. Admittedly / In light of the fact / As soon as

30. Which of the following choices best completes the sentence while maintaining the style?

> Bile acids created by the liver fragment fat molecules so other enzymes __________ can continue the dissolving of larger fat particles.

a. (breakers of fatty stuff)
b. (enzymes that are in the body)
c. (pancreatic and intestinal)
d. (acid and base)

31. Which of the following sentences would fit onto the end of the passage below and maintain the current style?

> Food enters the mouth and is broken down through the chewing process. The food is then swallowed and pushed into the esophagus. A process called peristalsis causes the food, now referred to as a bolus, to move down the esophagus to the stomach.

a. A little lid-like covering then opens up to allow the bolus to move into the stomach.
b. The lower esophageal sphincter then opens up to allow the bolus to move into the stomach.
c. The esophageal sphincter then pops open to let the food in.
d. Accordingly, the lower esophageal sphincter then moves to let things in the stomach.

32. Which of the following might be a good concluding statement for a research paper that linked proper nutrition to a healthy lifestyle?

a. In summary, food is important to our health. The food we eat passes through our digestive tract. The nutrition from that food affects the body.
b. In closing, people need to look more closely at the kinds of treats they are enjoying. Are we really ready to sacrifice healthy golden years for the sake of another cookie?
c. In summary, whole grains and fibrous vegetables are important additions to a balanced diet. They provide adequate fiber that pushes through the intestine. Water is also an important part of a healthy diet.
d. In conclusion, it's easy to see that foods like whole grains, fruit, and lean proteins can help maintain a healthy body by giving us the nutrients we need to function. A healthy diet will result in a longer, more enjoyable life.

33. Which of the following choices provides the best introduction to a story (introducing both character and plot)?

a. Jun wiped the phone and texted his father. He looked at the house again. Jun knew that the window wasn't supposed to look that way. They were all mostly the same, except for the big picture window that looked out over the lake. The lake stretched out behind the house. The sunlight sparkled on the clear water.
b. Jun wiped the sweat from his face. "Man, it's hot today. These summers are killer." He looked at the house again. Jun knew that the window wasn't supposed to look that way. He had spent the previous summer helping his father install all 27 windows on the old house. It had been a lot of work and the heat had been unrelenting.
c. Jun wiped the sweat from the phone and texted his father. Was his father up already? It was still early in the morning and his father had been working late again. Jun looked at the house again. Jun knew that the window wasn't supposed to look that way. He had spent the previous summer helping his father install all 27 windows on the old house.
d. Jun wiped the sweat from the phone and texted his father, "Breakfast is on the counter, Dad. Am at summerhouse now, be home before MiYoung's lesson." He looked at the house again. Jun knew that the window wasn't supposed to look that way. He had spent the previous summer helping his father install all 27 windows on the old house. Seeing the bent frame gripped his heart with fear. Someone had pried open the window recently. And that someone may still be in the basement.

34. Which of the following choices provides the best plot development? Complete the dialogue.

Fritz: "I saw Mary down in the art room today. Why was she there? I thought she quit Art Club."

Romerai: "She did. But something happened yesterday. I saw her after study hall and she was crying."

a. Fritz: "Ah, now it all fits. Justin told Mrs. Connors that Mary quit because of her two jobs."
Romerai: "Oh? You mean Mrs. Connors didn't know Mary was working to support her family?"
b. Fritz: "She's always crying about something. Besides, I feel like crying during study hall."
Romerai: "Yeah, study hall is so boring. I always finish all of my homework there."
c. Fritz: "Art Club is so much fun! Why would anyone want to quit?"
Romerai: "Maybe she had her reasons. But I can't imagine why she would quit in the middle of the pottery lesson."
d. Fritz: "Mrs. Connors must have talked to her about something. Art Club is her life!"
Romerai: "True, but Art Club isn't everyone else's life. There're other things, too."

35. Which of the following choices uses more than one technique to develop the plot?

a. Jun walked up the back porch and tightened his grip on the Louisville slugger. It felt light in his hands, much lighter than his heart. It was beating loudly in his ears as he took a step into the old farm kitchen.
b. Jun remembered the old farm kitchen well. He could still see his mother at the stove, cooking up something wonderful. That was before the cancer took her.
c. Jun slipped his fingers through the latch to the basement latch. He slipped into the semidarkness of the basement. On the top step, he heard something rustle below. "Come on out now! I know you're here!" Briefly, Jun's mind raced back to that horrible day he had found his mother at the bottom of the basement steps.
d. Suddenly, a large rat bolted from the darkness and scurried across the basement floor. It fled into a pile of wood in the corner. Jun relaxed his grip on the bat and blew air out between his teeth. His eyes searched the half-gloom of the basement, which now did not seem so terrifying.

36. Which of the following choices provides the best description?

a. The basement was coated in a light layer of dust. The old table saw sat quietly in the half-light.
b. A thin layer of dust was draped over the ancient table saw. A hot southern wind whipped some of the flower heads against the basement window, resulting in an eerie drumbeat.
c. Dust covered everything in the basement. The table saw was covered with dust. The wind blew outside. It was a loud sound.
d. Dust coated all of the stuff in the basement. Even the cobwebs were covered with dust. Outside, the wind blew more dust around in a small tornado.

37. Which of the following choices provides the best conclusion?

a. Jun heard a soft moan from the corner near the woodpile. He raised the bat and moved closer. There, bunched up on the floor, was a small girl. "Please don't hit me," she sobbed. "I was playing hide-and-seek with my friends. I pried the window open and climbed in. I didn't know it would shut on me!" Jun lowered the bat and helped the girl up. "Cassie! Your parents are so worried about you! You must have been here for two days!" Cassie nodded. "It was a good thing you have a refrigerator down here. I'm sorry, but I drank all of the soda you put in last week." Jun shook his head, relieved that Cassie had been found—and had been the one who opened the window.

b. Jun saw a little girl in the basement. She had been missing for two days. Her name was Cassie, and she was one of their neighbors. Cassie must have been playing hide-and-seek with her friends. Jun asked her and she said, "Yes." She looked very tired. She must have been tired, since she had been missing for two days. Her parents had called the police, and people were searching everywhere. Jun asked if she wanted something to eat. Cassie said that she didn't feel hungry because she had eaten the food from the basement refrigerator and freezer. Jun was just glad that it was Cassie who had broken into the house and not a real burglar.

c. "Jun! It's me, Cassie!" Jun looked into the corner. There was a small girl sitting against the wall. She looked really tired. She was surrounded by empty soda cans, ice-cream wrappers, and bags of potato chips. "Sorry, Jun! I got stuck in here. I was so hungry I ate everything you guys had in the fridge and freezer. By the way, you need to buy better ice cream. Those sandwiches gave me a stomachache." Jun shook his head. "Cassie, your parents have been looking for you for two days! They even called the police. I thought that a burglar broke in here. I don't care about the food. You're really lucky I came out here today. How would you have gotten out of the basement? The windows are too high up for you, and the door is latched at the top!"

d. Something rustled in the half-darkness of the basement, and Jun smelled a musty odor. A heap of rags began to move, and Jun raised the bat. Suddenly, a voice cried out. "Jun! It's me, Cassie! Don't hit me!" Jun lowered the bat. Cassie was one of the neighborhood kids. He saw her from time to time when he and his father went fishing over the summer. She was only around ten years old. What was she doing in the basement? He saw a pile of empty soda cans and ice-cream bar wrappers.

38. Which of the following sentences is the best choice for a topic sentence in a final research paper on *Macbeth*?

a. This research paper is about how Macbeth and his wife deal with guilt. It will talk about guilt in the play. It will cover how Shakespeare thought of guilt.

b. Macbeth is a complicated play with a variety of important themes; some of these themes deal with ambition and guilt in regards to the human condition.

c. Shakespeare's Macbeth is an insightful adventure into the nature of the human spirit; Macbeth and his wife are case studies for understanding various concepts.

d. One of the major themes in Macbeth revolves around guilt and how people manage it; this paper will address several examples of how Shakespeare illustrates the human condition and its relationship with guilt.

39. Your teacher would like you to rewrite the sentence below to make it more effective. Which of the following choices is an effective rewrite?

Peter who had struggled with dyslexia for years, finally was able to read on his own much to his own delight and the happiness of his own parents.

a. Peter had struggled with dyslexia. He was able to read. His parents were really happy for him.
b. Peter who had struggled with dyslexia for years; finally ,was able to read on his own—much to his own delight and the happiness of his own parents.
c. Peter, who had struggled with dyslexia for years, finally was able to read on his own; much to his own delight and the happiness of his own parents.
d. Peter, who had struggled with dyslexia for years, was finally able to read on his own. He was delighted and his parents were happy.

40. Your current events project is to develop a webpage about the issues in the Middle East. Which of the following choices would help create a dynamic page with current information?

a. a weekly blog about issues in the Middle East
b. an essay written about Middle Eastern customs
c. a newsfeed that updates in real-time
d. a link to a website about Middle Eastern issues

41. You have been assigned a research project on the structure of a certain enzyme that aids in protein digestion. However, the topic is too narrow and you need to broaden it. Which of the following choices is an effective topic that incorporates your original topic?

a. nutritional aids and digestion
b. digestion and people
c. how enzymes work in digestion
d. understanding the human body

42. In *The Communist Manifesto*, Karl Marx argues that the overthrow of the capitalist system is the only way to ensure that wealth is distributed fairly to the masses. Which of the following choices provides an example that would support the opposite point of view?

a. the poverty that exists on the streets of America and the wealth that can be found in Washington DC
b. the economic disparity between the Communist Chinese government and people in the countryside
c. the welfare problems that plague Great Britain and the manner in which the royal family lives
d. the high cost of living in South Korea compared to the extreme poverty found in North Korea

43. If your class is going to have a discussion on capitalism and communism, which of the following choices would best prepare you?

a. Karl Marx's The Communist Manifesto and Mao Tse Tung's "little red book"
b. Adam Smith's An Inquiry into the Nature and Causes of the Wealth of Nations and Alex de Toqueville's Democracy in America
c. R. Massie's Catherine the Great and E. Metaxas's Bonhoeffer
d. Karl Marx's The Communist Manifesto and Adam Smith's An Inquiry into the Nature and Causes of the Wealth of Nations

Read the following selection from Patrick Henry's address to the Virginia Convention in 1775 to answer questions 44–51:

No man thinks more highly than I do of the patriotism, as well as abilities, of the very worthy gentlemen who have just addressed the House. But different men often see the same subject in different lights; and, therefore, I hope it will not be thought disrespectful to those gentlemen if, entertaining as I do opinions of a character very opposite to theirs, I shall speak forth my sentiments freely and without reserve. This is no time for ceremony. The question before the House is one of awful moment to this country. For my own part, I consider it as nothing less than a question of freedom or slavery; and in proportion to the magnitude of the subject ought to be the freedom of the debate. It is only in this way that we can hope to arrive at the truth, and fulfill the great responsibility which we hold to God and our country. Should I keep back my opinions at such a time, through fear of giving offense, I should consider myself as guilty of treason towards my country, and of an act of disloyalty toward the Majesty of Heaven, which I revere above all earthly kings.

...

I have but one lamp by which my feet are guided, and that is the lamp of experience. I know of no way of judging of the future but by the past. And judging by the past, I wish to know what there has been in the conduct of the British ministry for the last ten years to justify those hopes with which gentlemen have been pleased to solace themselves and the House. Is it that insidious smile with which our petition has been lately received?

Trust it not, sir; it will prove a snare to your feet. Suffer not yourselves to be betrayed with a kiss. Ask yourselves how this gracious reception of our petition comports with those warlike preparations which cover our waters and darken our land. Are fleets and armies necessary to a work of love and reconciliation? Have we shown ourselves so unwilling to be reconciled that force must be called in to win back our love? Let us not deceive ourselves, sir. These are the implements of war and subjugation; the last arguments to which kings resort. I ask gentlemen, sir, what means this martial array, if its purpose be not to force us to submission? Can gentlemen assign any other possible motive for it? Has Great Britain any enemy, in this quarter of the world, to call for all this accumulation of navies and armies? No, sir, she has none. They are meant for us: they can be meant for no other. They are sent over to bind and rivet upon us those chains which the British ministry have been so long forging. And what have we to oppose to them? Shall we try argument? Sir, we have been trying that for the last ten years. Have we anything new to offer upon the subject? Nothing. We have held the subject up in every light of which it is capable; but it has been all in vain. Shall we resort to entreaty and humble supplication? What terms shall we find which have not been already exhausted? Let us not, I beseech you, sir, deceive ourselves. Sir, we have done everything that could be done to avert the storm which is now coming on. We have petitioned; we have remonstrated; we have supplicated; we have prostrated ourselves before the throne, and have implored its interposition to arrest the tyrannical hands of the ministry and Parliament. Our petitions have been slighted; our remonstrances have produced additional violence and insult; our supplications have been disregarded; and we have been spurned, with contempt, from the foot of the throne! In vain, after these things, may we indulge the fond hope of peace and reconciliation.

There is no longer any room for hope. If we wish to be free—if we mean to preserve inviolate those inestimable privileges for which we have been so long contending—if we mean not basely to abandon the noble struggle in which we have been so long engaged, and which we have pledged ourselves never to abandon until the glorious object of our contest shall be obtained—we must fight! I repeat it, sir, we must fight! An appeal to arms and to the God of hosts is all that is left us! They tell us, sir, that we are weak; unable to cope with so formidable an adversary. But when shall we be stronger? Will it be the next week, or the next year? Will it be when we are totally disarmed, and when a British guard shall be stationed in every house? Shall we gather strength by irresolution and inaction? Shall we acquire the means of effectual resistance by lying supinely on our backs and hugging the delusive phantom of hope, until our enemies shall have bound us hand and foot? Sir, we are not weak if we make a proper use of those means which the God of nature hath placed in our power. The millions of people, armed in the holy cause of liberty, and in such a country as that which we possess, are invincible by any force which our enemy can send against us. Besides, sir, we shall not fight our battles alone. There is a just God who presides over the destinies of nations, and who will raise up friends to fight our battles for us. The battle, sir, is not to the strong alone; it is to the vigilant, the active, the brave. Besides, sir, we have no election. If we were base enough to desire it, it is now too late to retire from the contest. There is no retreat but in submission and slavery! Our chains are forged! Their clanking may be heard on the plains of Boston! The war is inevitable—and let it come! I repeat it, sir, let it come.

It is in vain, sir, to extentuate the matter. Gentlemen may cry, Peace, Peace—but there is no peace. The war is actually begun! The next gale that sweeps from the north will bring to our ears the clash of resounding arms! Our brethren are already in the field! Why stand we here idle? What is it that gentlemen wish? What would they have? Is life so dear, or peace so sweet, as to be purchased at the price of chains and slavery? Forbid it, Almighty God! I know not what course others may take; but as for me, give me liberty or give me death!

44. Which of the following statements best illustrates the idea that Patrick Henry is willing to sacrifice his life in a cause he believes in?

a. In vain, after these things, may we indulge the fond hope of peace and reconciliation.
b. And what have we to oppose to them? Shall we try argument? Sir, we have been trying that for the last ten years.
c. I know not what course others may take; but as for me, give me liberty or give me death!
d. The battle, sir, is not to the strong alone; it is to the vigilant, the active, the brave.

45. Which of the following choices provides the best summary of the speech?

a. We appear to be fools to the King of England, who laughs at our petitions. We are going to lose our freedom and liberty if we consistently bow to his demands. We answer to a higher power than the King of England, and should make sure we are doing the right thing for ourselves and our people.
b. Despite repeated attempts at reconciliation with Britain, the breach between the people of the colonies and the throne of England cannot be repaired. The war with Britain has already started, and we need to answer the call to arms to preserve our liberty and freedom.
c. We are suffering the tyranny of Parliament. We have constantly petitioned and sued for peace, but the government has repeatedly rebuffed our advances. We have a big problem on our hands now, since there does not seem to be a hope of reconciliation.
d. People here should not love their lives so much that they are willing to give up basic human rights and dignities. We have already tried to discuss this matter with the government and our petitions have been repeatedly ignored.

46. How does Patrick Henry build support for his idea that the government is not respecting the pleas from the colonies?

a. He builds support by telling his listeners that he is ready to die for his beliefs.
b. He mentions that war is already brewing, and it is just a matter of fighting the war.
c. He builds support by asking if people love their peace more than their freedom.
d. He mentions that he is basing his ideas on his experience.

47. To whom is Patrick Henry referring when he mentions the "Majesty of Heaven"?

a. the president
b. the king
c. the parliament
d. God

48. How does Patrick Henry develop the idea that the only option for the colonies is to fight?

a. He mentions that this is not the time to stand on ceremony, that he must speak plainly, and that it is necessary for him to treat the subject as a matter of freedom or slavery.
b. He notes that their peace attempts have been rebuffed, they have been laughed at, and their rights have been trampled; they must fight for their liberty and freedom.
c. He shows that experience is his guide and that it has proven that the government does not have their best interests at heart; they must find another way to solve the problem.
d. He indicates that the men gathered at the convention are of a noble mind, although they may have differing ideas.

49. Which of the following choices best expresses Patrick Henry's point of view?

a. He feels that the possibility of reconciliation with the throne still lies within reach as long as people are open to communication.
b. He thinks that the colonies should attempt to understand the way the government views the colonies in light of their attempts to express their concerns.
c. He feels that noble people everywhere will understand what basic human freedoms and liberties are.
d. He thinks that the time for trying to reconcile with the ruling powers has passed and that people everywhere need to take sides in the war.

50. When Patrick Henry bases his ideas on past experience, can it be said that his reasoning is valid?

a. Yes, he supports his claim that the government is not going to alter its course by showing that past events indicate how it feels about colonial concerns.
b. No, he creates a straw man; he takes one idea from the opposing side and distorts it so he may argue against it.
c. Yes, he appeals to people's deepest feelings about themselves in asking whether they wish to fight for freedom or live in peace as slaves.
d. No, he bases his ideas on a faulty premise, that is, it is not reasonable to base ideas of what has happened in the past to determine what will happen in the future.

51. The movie *The Patriot* is about a man who is drawn into fighting the revolutionary war for his family. How does this compare to the ideas expressed in Patrick Henry's speech?

a. The ideas expressed in The Patriot revolve around the common man and his bravery, while the speech caters to arguments between states.
b. In both cases, the ideas expressed have little to do with what is happening in everyday life; rather, most of the tyrannies are occurring in the upper levels of government.
c. In both mediums, the participants express their strong desire for freedom and liberty over tyranny and oppression.
d. The main reason for fighting the war becomes apparent in both the speech and the movie: the freedom of slaves.

52. Your team needs to work together on a project. Each person needs to contribute and speak in the oral presentation. Which of the following choices could best help your group organize to accomplish this goal?

a. a chart listing all of the team members with their parts of the project, including multiple deadlines
b. periodic emails reminding team members of their need for a commitment
c. a meeting in which team members decide what part of the project they want to work on
d. graphs showing the productivity of each team member as well as the project deadline

53. You are at a town hall meeting about building a new park. Some voters want to raise taxes to pay for it, and others want to find different ways to get the money. Which of the following choices would be one question you could ask during a discussion to move the conversation forward?

a. It's ridiculous to say that we need to raise taxes just to get money for the new park. How can you people even think that way?
b. Since it is obvious the only real answer is to raise taxes, the real question is by how great of a percentage.
c. It may be necessary to raise taxes for this issue. However, what do we do when we have another important project that comes up?
d. While I understand the need to raise funds for the new park, are there other ways to raise money than just raising taxes?

54. The following statements were made by several of your classmates in a discussion on providing universal government health care. Which of the following choices synthesizes the ideas and draws a conclusion?

Abner: We need the government to step in and manage health care because hospital bills are too expensive.

Mauri: Government health care would mean that politicians now control what care and medicines you have access to.

Ping: Insurance companies deny too many people coverage. Government health care sounds like it would be good because everyone gets insurance. But then you just have the government denying care.

a. This debate is about health care. It seems that we need the government to help manage the rising costs of health care so everyone has access. We also need to deal with the unfair practices of insurance companies. If the government manages health care, everyone will be covered and be able to go to the hospital whenever they are sick.
b. According to the debate so far, rising hospital costs and insurance problems are good reasons to get the government involved in health care. However, the government will then control a big part of your life and can deny certain treatments. It seems like there are many pros and cons here: we must decide what we want to give up: some of our access to health care or some of our liberties.
c. According to the speakers here, the government control of health care is full of downsides. No one wants to pay a lot of money for health care, but that's only one problem. When the government manages something, it all comes down to politicians controlling what you can and can't have or do. What happens when politicians decide they won't cover expensive treatments for your dying mother? Or what if they decide everyone must eat broccoli?
d. It seems that there are different points of view here. If the government controls health care, it might affect the rising costs. Everyone would have access to health care. However, politicians would control all aspects of health care, too. Insurance companies are not allowing people to get coverage. However, the government may decide that people should not have certain medicines.

55. You are doing a short presentation for your science class. You need to show that the amount of rain that has fallen in the last two months is considerably less than what has fallen in the prior year. Which of the following choices makes the best use of digital media to convey your data?

a. An interactive software program that allows audience members to input data points onto a graphic and draw a graph based on audience data.
b. A ten-minute Internet video about the lack of rain that has fallen in the area and why it is causing problems for the local farmers and wildlife.
c. A section from a recent news article that discusses the lack of rainfall in the local area and the urgent need for rain. The article is two pages of text that includes quotes from local officials and scientists concerned with the environment.
d. A graph with the amount of rainfall on one axis and the month on the other axis: the data points are marked on the graph. It has two differently colored lines (blue for last year, red for this year) that run through the data points showing the various amounts of rainfall in each month.

56. The Parent-Teacher Organization at your school is giving a scholarship based on the best speech. Which of the following choices best illustrates formal language suitable to such a presentation, as well as developing a topic?

a. It's no joke that studying abroad is good for your brain—scientists have recently put together some stats showing that students who go overseas are better off than the ones that lay around at home. It's not just that they get to know other places and other kinds of people. It's also that they have better graduation rates. Not too bad a result for one semester in Brazil, right?

b. Does studying abroad enhance a student's academic experience? Recent studies certainly support this idea. Not only do students who study abroad develop a better cultural understanding of both the foreign country and their homeland, but they also have higher graduation rates than students who remain at home.

c. Is it a quantifiable fact that students who study abroad are better off than their home-bound peers? It is certainly true that a good number of students who intend to study abroad are interested in everything except their studies. But is it fair to disallow students from pursuing this endeavor simply in light of the fact that the motive is skewed?

d. I would like to thank the members of the PTO for assembling this evening. The opportunity to give a speech here is truly a great gift. This evening, I would like to discuss the nature of study abroad programs. Some of you may be wondering about the nature of study abroad programs. What I am going to talk about is probably quite different from what you are thinking.

Answers and Explanations

ELA-Literacy.L.9-10.1a

1. C: The new phone can perform a large number of tasks quickly, precisely, and efficiently.

Parallel structure in a sentence means to use consistent word patterns (like matching verb tenses). The sentence needs to be consistent throughout. Choice A is just a sentence with no parallel structure. Choices B and D are incorrect uses of the structure: incorrect verb tenses (B) and incorrect adverbs (D).

ELA-Literacy.L.9-10.1b

2. A: Unless you find a new partner

This is an example of a conditional adverbial clause; it acts like an adverb and usually starts with words like *if* or *unless*. This talks about a situation that could happen. The other choices do not make sense in this situation: it's clear from the second part of the sentence that a consequence is coming. Choices B and C are independent clauses, and choice D is a clause of manner.

ELA-Literacy.L.9-10.2a

3. A: I packed a picnic to take to the park with my friends; I made sure that I brought all of the plates and cups, too.

A semicolon is used to connect two independent clauses that are closely related. A comma should not be used to separate independent clauses as a comma is more for a pause in the text. The sentence needs some punctuation, so choice C is incorrect. Choice D uses a colon, which should be used to show a list or provide an explanation.

ELA-Literacy.L.9-10.2b

4. D: to the important ideal laid out by Patrick Henry: "Give me liberty, or give me death."

A colon can be used to show that a list or a quotation is coming next. Choice A uses a semicolon, which is best used for connecting independent clauses. Choice B is asking a question, and Choice C does not have the right punctuation.

ELA-Literacy.L.9-10.2c

5. B: sureptitious

This word should be spelled with 2 *r*'s: surreptitious. It means something that is secret or sly.

ELA-Literacy.L.9-10.3a

6. B: Smith, John. *Reason and Thought in the Modern Age*. Chicago: Juggernaut, 2010. Print.

MLA Style dictates that the general format for a citation is:

Author's last name, Author's first name. *The Title of Book in Italics*. City of Publication: Name of the Publisher, Year of Publication. Medium of Publication (Print, digital, etc.).

ELA-Literacy.L.9-10.4a

7. C: rancorous

Acrimonious means "bitter" or "vitriolic," and is very similar in meaning to *rancorous.*

ELA-Literacy.L.9-10.4b

8. B: interpretation, evolution, interpret

This question deals with being able to identify different meanings or parts of speech through patterns in words. The first and second blanks require nouns; the third blank requires a verb. Choice A provides noun, verb, verb. Choice C provides verb, noun, noun. Choice D provides all nouns.

ELA-Literacy.L.9-10.4c

9. B: It was derived from Latin and French.

The etymology of the word is the word's history, or where it came from. Here, the definition shows that it was from a Latin word meaning "he has chosen" and a French word (*eligere*) meaning "to choose."

ELA-Literacy.L.9-10.4d

10. D: a judicial statement

By using the dictionary definition above, it is easy to see that the elegit refers to a special kind of judicial statement. Choices A and B are tricky, but can be discounted through the context of the sentence. Choice C would not allow for the seizure of property.

ELA-Literacy.L.9-10.5a

11. A: oxymoron

Oxymorons use two seemingly nonrelated words to create a new term. The term "open secret" refers to the fact that the program is supposedly secret and frequently denied, but already well-known. Choice B is a statement that seems contradictory but actually may be true. Choice C is a word used to mimic a vocal sound. Choice D is a word that literally means one thing, but is used to refer to something different.

ELA-Literacy.L.9-10.5b

12. B: scrawny

This question is about analyzing the shades of meaning between similar words. Choices A and D are very positive words for being skinny. Choice C is an almost neutral term, but it leans more toward a positive bent. However, since everything else on the farm was in bad shape, the chicken was no doubt in a wretched condition—scrawny.

ELA-Literacy.L.9-10.6

13. D: I publish these essays at the present time for a particular reason, Eugenics, greatly grieved, not irrelevant

These words and phrases are key to the understanding of the selection. They identify the subject, why the topic is being written about, and the outcome of the project. While the other choices offer phrases taken from the same selection, you could not read them and get an idea about the nature of the passage, namely, that Chesterton felt that Eugenics was evil and that he needed to publish a work explaining why.

ELA-Literacy.RL.9-10.1

14. C: At least we'll die with harness on our back.

Macbeth explicitly states that he thinks that there is a chance they will die. Choice A refers to the outside forces working, Choice B refers to a death threat made to the messenger, and Choice D refers to the death of Lady Macbeth.

ELA-Literacy.RL.9-10.2

15. B: the destruction of the soul through the unbridled pursuit of power

Macbeth's pursuit of power knows no bounds and eventually leads to his destruction. Choice A is not mentioned in Macbeth, Choice C is too vague of an answer, and Choice D refers to another of Shakespeare's plays (*A Midsummer Night's Dream*).

ELA-Literacy.RL.9-10.3

16. A: He begins as a noble, loyal hero of land and becomes a murderer who understands the outcome of his actions.

In the beginning of the play, Macbeth is praised as a war hero who has helped the kingdom. He, however, becomes consumed with power. This pursuit of power eventually results in the destruction of everything that matters in his life: his marriage, his friendships, and even the kingdom that he sought to hold on to. Choice B is only partially correct (he is a murderer). Choice C is the opposite of what happens in the play, and Choice D is too vague.

ELA-Literacy.RL.9-10.4

17. C: Life is dark and fleeting.

Macbeth has just received word that his wife, the queen, is dead. He is ruminating on life. Choice A does not come from the context, Choice B is too literal of a reading, and Choice D is an incomplete answer.

ELA-Literacy.RL.9-10.5

18. D: the scene where Macbeth sees Banquo's ghost

Macbeth's uneasiness over the murder of his friend Banquo is manifested in this scene, and it creates tension in the play. It serves to show Macbeth's inner feelings and gives the noblemen cause to rise up against Macbeth (the turning point). Choice A only shows Lady Macbeth's inner turmoil, Choice B does not build tension in the story, and Choice C comes at a time when Macbeth is already accepting of the circumstance—it does not serve to create tension and it is not a turning point.

ELA-Literacy.RL.9-10.6

19. B: Rulers in both systems require the support of the immediate members of the government or ruling class in order to govern effectively.

In the US, the president is an elected official and needs to work with Congress. In Shakespeare's *Macbeth*, the king needs the support of the noblemen to rule effectively. Choice A only refers to a kingdom, Choice C refers to a democracy, and Choice D refers to neither.

ELA-Literacy.RL.9-10.7

20. A: The depiction of the sisters in the painting is different from that in the play, since the women have beards in the play and are hairless in the painting.

The painting by Fuseli shows three unattractive women with their arms extended. They look somewhat confused. The play itself mentions that Banquo cannot decide if the three are women because they all have beards. Choice B is not mentioned in the quote above nor shown in the painting, Choice C is wrong because Banquo is not shown in the painting, and Choice D is incorrect because Banquo mentions the women look like men. The painting does not depict them as monsters.

ELA-Literacy.RL.9-10.9

21. B: Judas Iscariot, the man who betrayed Jesus in the New Testament

The Bible has had an enormous amount of impact on Western writing, and Shakespeare is no different. Here, Macbeth is about to kill the king, a man who trusted Macbeth. This particular quote may be a reference to the story related in the New Testament, John 13, where Jesus is betrayed by one of His close friends and followers, Judas Iscariot. Jesus tells the man to do what he needs to do quickly ("Now after the piece of bread, Satan entered him. Then Jesus said to him, "What you do, do quickly." (NKJV, biblegateway.com)) Choice A is about Dante's guide during his trip through three domains (Virgil does not betray or murder the traveler). Choice C is about the king who created a tricky device to fool his enemies, and the Choice D is about a woman who wrote about the struggles of being at home while her husband was away.

ELA-Literacy.W.9-10.1a

22. C: Texting while driving is one of the key issues facing young people today: it's a fact that texting drivers have killed over 16,000 people between 2002 and 2007. While some people claim that any kind of distracted driving is dangerous, texting beats them all by keeping attention away from the road.

This choice is the only one that takes a clear stand on the issue and provides a counterargument. The other choices are either too vague (A and D) or do not provide a counterargument.

ELA-Literacy.W.9-10.1b

23. D: Texting while driving is more dangerous than driving while eating or talking on the phone because the driver's eyes are no longer on the road.

This provides a counterclaim with supporting evidence. Choice A actually supports the main claim. Choice B does not provide a counterargument: it changes the subject. Choice C provides a counterclaim but does not support it.

ELA-Literacy.W.9-10.1c

24. B: crack down on it—it's seen / But / according to

These phrases and words best complete the passage. Sentence one shows that there is more surprising information coming. The next sentence shows there is a change in the direction, so words like *but* or *however* are needed. Finally, a dependent clause explains more to the reader

ELA-Literacy.W.9-10.1d

25. B: No one likes distracted drivers. They are not that smart. They could kill someone. They don't think about others.

Choice B is inappropriate for a report; the style is too simple and choppy. The information contained in the sentences is more emotional than factual. The other choices would all be able to be a part of a formal paper, since they are more grade appropriate in style and supporting content.

ELA-Literacy.W.9-10.1e

26. A: While it's clear that distracted driving in any form is dangerous, texting while driving is particularly lethal. It is now up to citizens to organize an effective method for managing this practice while balancing individual rights.

This choice provides a clear concluding statement that supports the argument and gives a balanced call to action. Choice B is vague and does not offer a closing statement. Choice C is too informal and only offers new information. Choice D supplies information that may have been in the main text but does not wrap it up with a call to action.

ELA-Literacy.W.9-10.2a

27. A: Include an introductory paragraph about the process of digestion and how it relates to nutrition. Include a heading showing that it is the introduction and a graphic illustrating a person eating.

This is the best choice because it introduces a topic (and identifies it with a heading), organizes the ideas, and uses a graphic to give the reader an idea about the content. Choice B is too specific, Choice C uses too many graphics for a research paper, and Choice D does not supply a good introduction and does not use any graphics to explain the process.

ELA-Literacy.W.9-10.2b

28. C: "The simple fact of the matter is, you are what you eat," noted nutritionist Danny Kaye.

A nutritionist would be qualified to issue a quote on the topic at hand. He supplies new information by stating the obvious: you are what you eat. Choice A is not appropriate because it provides no new information; we also do not know what kind of professor the man is. Choice B does not provide any new information, and the speaker is not a qualified scientist. Choice D is an opinion given by a non-expert, which is not fit for a research paper.

ELA-Literacy.W.9-10.2c

29. D: Admittedly / In light of the fact / As soon as

These words best complete the selection by providing the correct transitions in the paragraph. Transitions provide an important part of any writing because they help clarify ideas and relationships in the passage. Choice A acts as if this is a conclusion paragraph—it's not, which can be seen in the way the ideas begin to broaden and expand. Choice B provides a sequence, but the passage is clearly not a list of items or ideas. Choice C does not provide the correct direction for the ideas.

ELA-Literacy.W.9-10.2d

30. C: (pancreatic and intestinal)

This choice provides the best answer because it maintains the formal style of the sentence. Choice A is too informal. Choice B does not provide any information and so does not belong in parentheses. Choice D has nothing to do with the topic.

ELA-Literacy.W.9-10.2e

31. B: The lower esophageal sphincter then opens up to allow the bolus to move into the stomach.

This choice preserves the formal style and vocabulary used to illustrate the process. Each word is chosen precisely to convey the actual action. Choice A does not use the correct vocabulary. Choice C is too informal. Choice D does not give the reader a detailed idea of what is going into the stomach.

ELA-Literacy.W.9-10.2f

32. D: In conclusion, it's easy to see that foods like whole grains, fruit, and lean proteins can help maintain a healthy body by giving us the nutrients we need to function. A healthy diet will result in a longer, more enjoyable life.

This conclusion maintains a formal style and provides information that links good eating habits to longer life. Choice A describes the process, Choice B does not provide any information that may help the reader understand what was in the passage, and Choice C gives too many details without drawing any conclusions.

ELA-Literacy.W.9-10.3a

33. D: Jun wiped the sweat from the phone and texted his father, "Breakfast is on the counter, Dad. Am at summerhouse now, be home before MiYoung's lesson." He looked at the house again. Jun knew that the window wasn't supposed to look that way. He had spent the previous summer helping his father install all 27 windows on the old house. Seeing the bent frame gripped his heart with fear. Someone had pried open the window recently. And that someone may still be in the basement.

This choice is a good one because it introduces a problem (someone has broken into the summerhouse), and tells you about the main character (he is responsible, helpful, and hardworking.) The other choices do not develop both character and problem. Choice A provides description but does not develop the plot. Choice B provides some character development but no plot. Choice C introduces the problem but does not develop it.

ELA-Literacy.W.9-10.3b

34. A: Fritz: "Ah, now it all fits. Justin told Mrs. Connors that Mary quit because of her two jobs."

Romerai: "Oh? You mean Mrs. Connors didn't know Mary was working to support her family?"

This choice best develops the story because it allows us to see that there is a problem (Mary quit Art Club) and some plot development (she has been working two jobs to help support her family). Now she is probably discussing the issue with the teacher in the art room. The other choices do not provide any real plot development or only contain empty conversations.

ELA-Literacy.W.9-10.3c

35. C: Jun slipped his fingers through the latch to the basement latch. He slipped into the semidarkness of the basement. On the top step, he heard something rustle below. "Come on out now! I know you're here!" Briefly, Jun's mind raced back to that horrible day he had found his mother at the bottom of the basement steps.

This choice is the best because it uses narration, a monologue, and a flashback to develop the plot. Choices A and D only use narration, while Choice B uses a flashback.

ELA-Literacy.W.9-10.3d

36. B: A thin layer of dust was draped over the ancient table saw. A hot southern wind whipped some of the flower heads against the basement window, resulting in an eerie drumbeat.

This choice provides the best description because it uses sight, sound, and temperature. It is hot and windy; the flower heads are banging on the basement window and the whole basement is covered in dust. Choice A only provides sight description. Choice C provides sight and sound.

ELA-Literacy.W.9-10.3e

37. A: Jun heard a soft moan from the corner near the woodpile. He raised the bat and moved closer. There, bunched up on the floor, was a small girl. "Please don't hit me," she sobbed. "I was playing hide-and-seek with my friends. I pried the window open and climbed in. I didn't know it would shut on me!" Jun lowered the bat and helped the girl up. "Cassie! Your parents are so worried about you! You must have been here for two days!" Cassie nodded. "It was a good thing you have a refrigerator down here. I'm sorry, but I drank all of the soda you put in last week." Jun shook his head, relieved that Cassie had been found—and had been the one who opened the window.

This provides the most satisfactory conclusion to the story. It explains how the window was damaged and wraps up the story. Choice B provides an ending, but it is too brief and does not match the style of the prior narratives. Choices C and D do not provide an ending nor resolution to the problem in the story (Jun's opened window).

ELA-Literacy.W.9-10.4

38. D: One of the major themes in *Macbeth* revolves around guilt and how people manage it; this paper will address several examples of how Shakespeare illustrates the human condition and its relationship with guilt.

Choice D provides a good introduction to the topic because it tells you what will be discussed in the paper. It is also written at grade level and in an appropriate style. Choice A is informal and not written at a 10th-grade level. Choice B is too broad, and Choice C is too vague.

ELA-Literacy.W.9-10.5

39. D: Peter, who had struggled with dyslexia for years, was finally able to read on his own. He was delighted and his parents were happy.

This is the best choice here. The sentence is a run-on sentence that needs some punctuation. It also requires a way to set off the dependent clause (who had struggled with dyslexia for years). Choice A removes too much information and does not provide grade-appropriate writing. Choices B and C are grammatically incorrect.

ELA-Literacy.W.9-10.6

40. C: a newsfeed that updates in real-time

This choice would provide constantly updated information about the topic. Choice A would provide some new information, but only a weekly update may not be enough. Choice B is more about static traditions. Choice D makes users go to another site, which may or may not have updated information.

ELA-Literacy.W.9-10.7

41. C: how enzymes work in digestion

This is the best way to broaden the topic while still including the original one. Choice A is off-topic, Choice B is too broad, and Choice D is too vague.

ELA-Literacy.W.9-10.9b

42. B: the economic disparity between the Communist Chinese government and people in the countryside

This is the only choice that can provide support to an opposing viewpoint because it is the only one that illustrates the disparities in a communist society. Wealth is not equally distributed in China; the people in the city are much better off than those in the countryside. Members of the government are treated better than regular citizens, despite the obvious need of the impoverished. All of the other choices involved capitalist systems.

ELA-Literacy.SL.9-10.1a

43. D: Karl Marx's The Communist Manifesto and Adam Smith's An Inquiry into the Nature and Causes of the Wealth of Nations

These two books will give you insight into each side of the argument. Choice A would give you only an understanding of communism, Choice B would give you only an understanding of capitalism, and Choice C does not address the topic at hand.

ELA-Literacy.RI.9-10.1

44. C: I know not what course others may take; but as for me, give me liberty or give me death!

This quote from Henry was part of the urge to battle delivered in 1775. This statement supports the idea that Henry was willing to give his own life in the cause of war with Britain. The other choices all contribute to that idea, but none state it so clearly.

ELA-Literacy.RI.9-10.2

45. B: Despite repeated attempts at reconciliation with Britain, the breach between the people of the colonies and the throne of England cannot be repaired. The war with Britain has already started, and we need to answer the call to arms to preserve our liberty and freedom.

This is the best summary of the above passage. The other choices only provide a partial summary or are too vague.

ELA-Literacy.RI.9-10.3

46. D: He mentions that he is basing his ideas on his experience.

Henry illustrates his ideas by referring to past experience. He mentions that the colonies have repeatedly tried to work with the government, but they have been treated poorly. Choice A supports the idea that Henry is serious about the war. Choice B supports the idea that Henry thinks that the tipping point has already passed. Choice C is more of an attack on people's pride.

ELA-Literacy.RI.9-10.4

47. D: God

Patrick Henry is referring to his obligations to a higher power, or God. The other choices refer to people or institutions.

ELA-Literacy.RI.9-10.5

48. B: He notes that their peace attempts have been rebuffed, they have been laughed at, and their rights have been trampled; they must fight for their liberty and freedom.

Patrick Henry's entire speech is a call to arms. He creates support for his call to war by showing that the people have tried to discuss their problems and have been treated badly.

Choice A involves his introduction to his speech. Choice C is too vague and does not fully address the issue. Choice D only concerns the way he approaches his audience.

ELA-Literacy.RI.9-10.6

49. D: He thinks that the time for trying to reconcile with the ruling powers has passed and that people everywhere need to take sides in the war.

The entire speech is a call to arms. Patrick Henry notes that reconciliation attempts have been rebuffed, and they have been sneered at. The liberties of the people have been trampled on. In his view, the war has already begun. Choice A is the opposite of what he meant, Choice B is not supported by the text, and Choice C may be involved with his general pattern of thinking, but does not adequately express his point of view.

ELA-Literacy.RI.9-10.8

50. A: Yes, he supports his claim that the government is not going to alter its course by showing that past events indicate how it feels about colonial concerns.

Henry's reasoning from experience is a strong foundation for his argument. Choice B is incorrect because Henry is drawing on actual events. Choice C is wrong because the question asks about

Henry's development of his argument of past experience, not the actual appeal to his audience's better nature. Choice D is incorrect because it *is* logical to argue from past experience.

ELA-Literacy.RI.9-10.7

51. C: In both mediums, the participants express their strong desire for freedom and liberty over tyranny and oppression.

In the movie, the main character is fighting for his liberty and freedom, which matches the ideas expressed in the speech. The colonists were not fighting because they wanted to cause trouble, they were fighting because they were being heavily oppressed. Choices A and B are incorrect because the ideas are not found in both the speech and movie. Choice D is incorrect because the Revolutionary War was fought for independence, not the freedom of slaves (which happened during the Civil War).

ELA-Literacy.SL.9-10.1b

52. A: a chart listing all of the team members with their parts of the project, including multiple deadlines

This question is designed to help students understand how to organize and set clear goals. A chart with all the information on it and the deadlines would be a useful tool. Students could reference the chart at any time to see what they should be doing and when it is due. Choice

B is a good idea to use after the chart is developed. Choice C is necessary at the beginning but will not provide ongoing organizational assistance. Choice D is almost like a punishment—showing who is not working on their part of the project.

ELA-Literacy.SL.9-10.1c

53. D: While I understand the need to raise funds for the new park, are there other ways to raise money than just raising taxes?

This is the best choice because it acknowledges the other side of the argument in the discussion in a respectful way and moves the discussion forward by asking an open-ended question calling for ideas. Choice A insults people. Choice B completely dismisses the other side of the discussion. Choice C changes the topic.

ELA-Literacy.SL.9-10.1d

54. B: According to the debate so far, rising hospital costs and insurance problems are good reasons to get the government involved in health care. However, the government will then control a big part of your life and can deny certain treatments. It seems like there are many pros and cons here: we must decide what we want to give up: some of our access to health care or some of our liberties.

This choice puts together all of the ideas from the speakers and summarizes them. It then illustrates important parts of the argument and draws a conclusion. Choices A and C only provide one side of the argument. Choice D summarizes but does not draw any conclusions.

ELA-Literacy.SL.9-10.2

55. D: A graph with the amount of rainfall on one axis and the month on the other axis: the data points are marked on the graph. It has two differently colored lines (blue for last year, red for this year) that run through the data points showing the various amounts of rainfall in each month.

This is the most effective way to present your data to the audience. A simple, clear graphic like this shows the different amount of rain in each month and then allows the audience to see the trend with the lines connecting the data points. Choice A is incorrect because it allows for the audience to input its own data, which may or may not be accurate. Choice B is too long for a short presentation and does not illustrate the idea so that it will stay in your audience's mind. Choice C is too much text for a short presentation and does not help the audience get a visual representation of the data.

ELA-Literacy.SL.9-10.3

56. B: Does studying abroad enhance a student's academic experience? Recent studies certainly support this idea. Not only do students who study abroad develop a better cultural understanding of both the foreign country and their homeland, but they also have higher graduation rates than students who remain at home.

A presentation to the PTO must be a formal speech. This is the only example of a formal speech that develops a topic and begins to provide support for it in an acceptable manner. Choice A is too informal. Choice C is formal but does not introduce and develop one topic. Choice D is formal but does not develop an idea.

How to Overcome Test Anxiety

Just the thought of taking a test is enough to make most people a little nervous. A test is an important event that can have a long-term impact on your future, so it's important to take it seriously and it's natural to feel anxious about performing well. But just because anxiety is normal, that doesn't mean that it's helpful in test taking, or that you should simply accept it as part of your life. Anxiety can have a variety of effects. These effects can be mild, like making you feel slightly nervous, or severe, like blocking your ability to focus or remember even a simple detail.

If you experience test anxiety—whether severe or mild—it's important to know how to beat it. To discover this, first you need to understand what causes test anxiety.

Causes of Test Anxiety

While we often think of anxiety as an uncontrollable emotional state, it can actually be caused by simple, practical things. One of the most common causes of test anxiety is that a person does not feel adequately prepared for their test. This feeling can be the result of many different issues such as poor study habits or lack of organization, but the most common culprit is time management. Starting to study too late, failing to organize your study time to cover all of the material, or being distracted while you study will mean that you're not well prepared for the test. This may lead to cramming the night before, which will cause you to be physically and mentally exhausted for the test. Poor time management also contributes to feelings of stress, fear, and hopelessness as you realize you are not well prepared but don't know what to do about it.

Other times, test anxiety is not related to your preparation for the test but comes from unresolved fear. This may be a past failure on a test, or poor performance on tests in general. It may come from comparing yourself to others who seem to be performing better or from the stress of living up to expectations. Anxiety may be driven by fears of the future—how failure on this test would affect your educational and career goals. These fears are often completely irrational, but they can still negatively impact your test performance.

Elements of Test Anxiety

As mentioned earlier, test anxiety is considered to be an emotional state, but it has physical and mental components as well. Sometimes you may not even realize that you are suffering from test anxiety until you notice the physical symptoms. These can include trembling hands, rapid heartbeat, sweating, nausea, and tense muscles. Extreme anxiety may lead to fainting or vomiting. Obviously, any of these symptoms can have a negative impact on testing. It is important to recognize them as soon as they begin to occur so that you can address the problem before it damages your performance.

The mental components of test anxiety include trouble focusing and inability to remember learned information. During a test, your mind is on high alert, which can help you recall information and stay focused for an extended period of time. However, anxiety interferes with your mind's natural processes, causing you to blank out, even on the questions you know well. The strain of testing during anxiety makes it difficult to stay focused, especially on a test that may take several hours. Extreme anxiety can take a huge mental toll, making it difficult not only to recall test information but even to understand the test questions or pull your thoughts together.

Effects of Test Anxiety

Test anxiety is like a disease—if left untreated, it will get progressively worse. Anxiety leads to poor performance, and this reinforces the feelings of fear and failure, which in turn lead to poor performances on subsequent tests. It can grow from a mild nervousness to a crippling condition. If allowed to progress, test anxiety can have a big impact on your schooling, and consequently on your future.

Test anxiety can spread to other parts of your life. Anxiety on tests can become anxiety in any stressful situation, and blanking on a test can turn into panicking in a job situation. But fortunately, you don't have to let anxiety rule your testing and determine your grades. There are a number of relatively simple steps you can take to move past anxiety and function normally on a test and in the rest of life.

Physical Steps for Beating Test Anxiety

While test anxiety is a serious problem, the good news is that it can be overcome. It doesn't have to control your ability to think and remember information. While it may take time, you can begin taking steps today to beat anxiety.

Just as your first hint that you may be struggling with anxiety comes from the physical symptoms, the first step to treating it is also physical. Rest is crucial for having a clear, strong mind. If you are tired, it is much easier to give in to anxiety. But if you establish good sleep habits, your body and mind will be ready to perform optimally, without the strain of exhaustion. Additionally, sleeping well helps you to retain information better, so you're more likely to recall the answers when you see the test questions.

Getting good sleep means more than going to bed on time. It's important to allow your brain time to relax. Take study breaks from time to time so it doesn't get overworked, and don't study right before bed. Take time to rest your mind before trying to rest your body, or you may find it difficult to fall asleep.

Along with sleep, other aspects of physical health are important in preparing for a test. Good nutrition is vital for good brain function. Sugary foods and drinks may give a burst of energy but this burst is followed by a crash, both physically and emotionally. Instead, fuel your body with protein and vitamin-rich foods.

Also, drink plenty of water. Dehydration can lead to headaches and exhaustion, especially if your brain is already under stress from the rigors of the test. Particularly if your test is a long one, drink water during the breaks. And if possible, take an energy-boosting snack to eat between sections.

Along with sleep and diet, a third important part of physical health is exercise. Maintaining a steady workout schedule is helpful, but even taking 5-minute study breaks to walk can help get your blood pumping faster and clear your head. Exercise also releases endorphins, which contribute to a positive feeling and can help combat test anxiety.

When you nurture your physical health, you are also contributing to your mental health. If your body is healthy, your mind is much more likely to be healthy as well. So take time to rest, nourish your body with healthy food and water, and get moving as much as possible. Taking these physical steps will make you stronger and more able to take the mental steps necessary to overcome test anxiety.

Mental Steps for Beating Test Anxiety

Working on the mental side of test anxiety can be more challenging, but as with the physical side, there are clear steps you can take to overcome it. As mentioned earlier, test anxiety often stems from lack of preparation, so the obvious solution is to prepare for the test. Effective studying may be the most important weapon you have for beating test anxiety, but you can and should employ several other mental tools to combat fear.

First, boost your confidence by reminding yourself of past success—tests or projects that you aced. If you're putting as much effort into preparing for this test as you did for those, there's no reason you should expect to fail here. Work hard to prepare; then trust your preparation.

Second, surround yourself with encouraging people. It can be helpful to find a study group, but be sure that the people you're around will encourage a positive attitude. If you spend time with others who are anxious or cynical, this will only contribute to your own anxiety. Look for others who are motivated to study hard from a desire to succeed, not from a fear of failure.

Third, reward yourself. A test is physically and mentally tiring, even without anxiety, and it can be helpful to have something to look forward to. Plan an activity following the test, regardless of the outcome, such as going to a movie or getting ice cream.

When you are taking the test, if you find yourself beginning to feel anxious, remind yourself that you know the material. Visualize successfully completing the test. Then take a few deep, relaxing breaths and return to it. Work through the questions carefully but with confidence, knowing that you are capable of succeeding.

Developing a healthy mental approach to test taking will also aid in other areas of life. Test anxiety affects more than just the actual test—it can be damaging to your mental health and even contribute to depression. It's important to beat test anxiety before it becomes a problem for more than testing.

Study Strategy

Being prepared for the test is necessary to combat anxiety, but what does being prepared look like? You may study for hours on end and still not feel prepared. What you need is a strategy for test prep. The next few pages outline our recommended steps to help you plan out and conquer the challenge of preparation.

Step 1: Scope Out the Test

Learn everything you can about the format (multiple choice, essay, etc.) and what will be on the test. Gather any study materials, course outlines, or sample exams that may be available. Not only will this help you to prepare, but knowing what to expect can help to alleviate test anxiety.

Step 2: Map Out the Material

Look through the textbook or study guide and make note of how many chapters or sections it has. Then divide these over the time you have. For example, if a book has 15 chapters and you have five days to study, you need to cover three chapters each day. Even better, if you have the time, leave an extra day at the end for overall review after you have gone through the material in depth.

If time is limited, you may need to prioritize the material. Look through it and make note of which sections you think you already have a good grasp on, and which need review. While you are studying, skim quickly through the familiar sections and take more time on the challenging parts.

Write out your plan so you don't get lost as you go. Having a written plan also helps you feel more in control of the study, so anxiety is less likely to arise from feeling overwhelmed at the amount to cover.

Step 3: Gather Your Tools

Decide what study method works best for you. Do you prefer to highlight in the book as you study and then go back over the highlighted portions? Or do you type out notes of the important information? Or is it helpful to make flashcards that you can carry with you? Assemble the pens, index cards, highlighters, post-it notes, and any other materials you may need so you won't be distracted by getting up to find things while you study.

If you're having a hard time retaining the information or organizing your notes, experiment with different methods. For example, try color-coding by subject with colored pens, highlighters, or post-it notes. If you learn better by hearing, try recording yourself reading your notes so you can listen while in the car, working out, or simply sitting at your desk. Ask a friend to quiz you from your flashcards, or try teaching someone the material to solidify it in your mind.

Step 4: Create Your Environment

It's important to avoid distractions while you study. This includes both the obvious distractions like visitors and the subtle distractions like an uncomfortable chair (or a too-comfortable couch that makes you want to fall asleep). Set up the best study environment possible: good lighting and a comfortable work area. If background music helps you focus, you may want to turn it on, but otherwise keep the room quiet. If you are using a computer to take notes, be sure you don't have any other windows open, especially applications like social media, games, or anything else that could distract you. Silence your phone and turn off notifications. Be sure to keep water close by so you stay hydrated while you study (but avoid unhealthy drinks and snacks).

Also, take into account the best time of day to study. Are you freshest first thing in the morning? Try to set aside some time then to work through the material. Is your mind clearer in the afternoon or evening? Schedule your study session then. Another method is to study at the same time of day that you will take the test, so that your brain gets used to working on the material at that time and will be ready to focus at test time.

Step 5: Study!

Once you have done all the study preparation, it's time to settle into the actual studying. Sit down, take a few moments to settle your mind so you can focus, and begin to follow your study plan. Don't give in to distractions or let yourself procrastinate. This is your time to prepare so you'll be ready to fearlessly approach the test. Make the most of the time and stay focused.

Of course, you don't want to burn out. If you study too long you may find that you're not retaining the information very well. Take regular study breaks. For example, taking five minutes out of every hour to walk briskly, breathing deeply and swinging your arms, can help your mind stay fresh.

As you get to the end of each chapter or section, it's a good idea to do a quick review. Remind yourself of what you learned and work on any difficult parts. When you feel that you've mastered the material, move on to the next part. At the end of your study session, briefly skim through your notes again.

But while review is helpful, cramming last minute is NOT. If at all possible, work ahead so that you won't need to fit all your study into the last day. Cramming overloads your brain with more information than it can process and retain, and your tired mind may struggle to recall even previously learned information when it is overwhelmed with last-minute study. Also, the urgent nature of cramming and the stress placed on your brain contribute to anxiety. You'll be more likely to go to the test feeling unprepared and having trouble thinking clearly.

So don't cram, and don't stay up late before the test, even just to review your notes at a leisurely pace. Your brain needs rest more than it needs to go over the information again. In fact, plan to finish your studies by noon or early afternoon the day before the test. Give your brain the rest of the day to relax or focus on other things, and get a good night's sleep. Then you will be fresh for the test and better able to recall what you've studied.

Step 6: Take a Practice Test

Many courses offer sample tests, either online or in the study materials. This is an excellent resource to check whether you have mastered the material, as well as to prepare for the test format and environment.

Check the test format ahead of time: the number of questions, the type (multiple choice, free response, etc.), and the time limit. Then create a plan for working through them. For example, if you have 30 minutes to take a 60-question test, your limit is 30 seconds per question. Spend less time on the questions you know well so that you can take more time on the difficult ones.

If you have time to take several practice tests, take the first one open book, with no time limit. Work through the questions at your own pace and make sure you fully understand them. Gradually work up to taking a test under test conditions: sit at a desk with all study materials put away and set a timer. Pace yourself to make sure you finish the test with time to spare and go back to check your answers if you have time.

After each test, check your answers. On the questions you missed, be sure you understand why you missed them. Did you misread the question (tests can use tricky wording)? Did you forget the information? Or was it something you hadn't learned? Go back and study any shaky areas that the practice tests reveal.

Taking these tests not only helps with your grade, but also aids in combating test anxiety. If you're already used to the test conditions, you're less likely to worry about it, and working through tests until you're scoring well gives you a confidence boost. Go through the practice tests until you feel comfortable, and then you can go into the test knowing that you're ready for it.

Test Tips

On test day, you should be confident, knowing that you've prepared well and are ready to answer the questions. But aside from preparation, there are several test day strategies you can employ to maximize your performance.

First, as stated before, get a good night's sleep the night before the test (and for several nights before that, if possible). Go into the test with a fresh, alert mind rather than staying up late to study.

Try not to change too much about your normal routine on the day of the test. It's important to eat a nutritious breakfast, but if you normally don't eat breakfast at all, consider eating just a protein bar. If you're a coffee drinker, go ahead and have your normal coffee. Just make sure you time it so that the caffeine doesn't wear off right in the middle of your test. Avoid sugary beverages, and drink enough water to stay hydrated but not so much that you need a restroom break 10 minutes into the test. If your test isn't first thing in the morning, consider going for a walk or doing a light workout before the test to get your blood flowing.

Allow yourself enough time to get ready, and leave for the test with plenty of time to spare so you won't have the anxiety of scrambling to arrive in time. Another reason to be early is to select a good seat. It's helpful to sit away from doors and windows, which can be distracting. Find a good seat, get out your supplies, and settle your mind before the test begins.

When the test begins, start by going over the instructions carefully, even if you already know what to expect. Make sure you avoid any careless mistakes by following the directions.

Then begin working through the questions, pacing yourself as you've practiced. If you're not sure on an answer, don't spend too much time on it, and don't let it shake your confidence. Either skip it and come back later, or eliminate as many wrong answers as possible and guess among the remaining ones. Don't dwell on these questions as you continue—put them out of your mind and focus on what lies ahead.

Be sure to read all of the answer choices, even if you're sure the first one is the right answer Sometimes you'll find a better one if you keep reading. But don't second-guess yourself if you do immediately know the answer. Your gut instinct is usually right. Don't let test anxiety rob you of the information you know.

If you have time at the end of the test (and if the test format allows), go back and review your answers. Be cautious about changing any, since your first instinct tends to be correct, but make sure you didn't misread any of the questions or accidentally mark the wrong answer choice. Look over any you skipped and make an educated guess.

At the end, leave the test feeling confident. You've done your best, so don't waste time worrying about your performance or wishing you could change anything. Instead, celebrate the successful completion of this test. And finally, use this test to learn how to deal with anxiety even better next time.

Review Video: Test Anxiety
Visit mometrix.com/academy and enter code: 100340

Important Qualification

Not all anxiety is created equal. If your test anxiety is causing major issues in your life beyond the classroom or testing center, or if you are experiencing troubling physical symptoms related to your anxiety, it may be a sign of a serious physiological or psychological condition. If this sounds like your situation, we strongly encourage you to seek professional help.

Thank You

We at Mometrix would like to extend our heartfelt thanks to you, our friend and patron, for allowing us to play a part in your journey. It is a privilege to serve people from all walks of life who are unified in their commitment to building the best future they can for themselves.

The preparation you devote to these important testing milestones may be the most valuable educational opportunity you have for making a real difference in your life. We encourage you to put your heart into it—that feeling of succeeding, overcoming, and yes, conquering will be well worth the hours you've invested.

We want to hear your story, your struggles and your successes, and if you see any opportunities for us to improve our materials so we can help others even more effectively in the future, please share that with us as well. **The team at Mometrix would be absolutely thrilled to hear from you!** So please, send us an email (support@mometrix.com) and let's stay in touch.

If you'd like some additional help, check out these other resources we offer for your exam:
http://MometrixFlashcards.com/CCSS

Online Resources

Due to our efforts to try to keep this book to a manageable length, we've created a link that will give you access to all of your online resources:

mometrix.com/resources719/ccg10ela

It's Your Moment, Let's Celebrate It!

Share your story @mometrixtestpreparation